'This is an extraordinary book: an anatomy of an abusive relationship, harrowing but leavened by love, a deep belief in the power of words and the wisdom earned through decades of reflection. It is, in the end, a story of healing. Inspirational.'
Tom Bullough, author of *Sarn Helen*

'*Nightshade Mother* is a compelling and heartbreaking read, the daughter going to extremes of forbearance to be kind, loving and rigorously honest in her portrait of the abusive and destructive mother. An astonishing feat of reclamation of a childhood, the adult writer guiding her child self, right up to her mother's death. Gwyneth Lewis has plumbed the depths of familial harm with courage and grace, giving us all hope that it's possible to transcend circumstance.'
Pascale Petit, author of *Mama Amazonica*

'What sort of parenting can make an adult, decades on, feel like "a trespasser in their own life"? In this unsparing memoir of a passionately controlling mother, who needs to keep a gifted child in her place, Gwyneth Lewis explores the nature of the damage done, the discovery of patchy but real vehicles of healing, the challenges of where and how to offer – or to postpone – forgiveness. All this is done with authority and (in the best sense) dispassion – not chill, not absent feeling, but clarity in and about feeling. It is a moving, difficult, and, ultimately, loving record, insisting on growing beyond both collusion and resentment.'
Rowan Williams, author of *Tokens of Trust*

'How do we flourish when our early nurture is also an experience of profound harm? Compelling, radical and moving, Gwyneth Lewis's extraordinary memoir is a revelatory journey back to the self she was never allowed to be. Documenting growing up speaking Welsh in the cultural heartlands of Welsh language renaissance, she finds in that Eden also a place of torture. Daughter of a "nightshade mother", whose complex care unwittingly made open prisons of her childhood and adolescence, Gwyneth Lewis writes her way back to freedom and sanity through engagement with places of love and joy following a path that will resonate with, and inspire, many of us.'
alice hiller, author of *bird of winter*

'This is an astonishing memoir. It is remarkable, the combination of unrelenting clarity and straightforwardness, and the subtlety of all the insidious and insistent terror (and rage) described. The book seems to me a triumph of tone and poise amidst so much disarray and confusion. It floats free of the by now all too familiar Sanity, Madness and the Family accounts of devastated childhoods. It's utterly free of sentimentality and special pleading – and shows us something partly explained by plain and lucid and understatedly poetic description. It seems to me extraordinary that Gwyneth Lewis is more than able to write this unique version of the growth of the poet's mind. We are all failures because we fail to cure our parents; this book shows the terrible impossibility of the founding task of everyone's life.'
Adam Phillips, psychoanalyst and author of *The Beast in the Nursery*

'*Nightshade Mother* is a mesmerising book. It is both an unflinchingly honest account of toxic motherhood, offering understanding without easy forgiveness, and a compelling story of becoming a poet. Gwyneth Lewis weaves a unique, multi-layered narrative, putting her childhood diaries side by side with adult recollections, as if to test the fallibility of memory. Her frugal parents threw nothing away believing that each scrap may become useful. Indeed, as she disentangles her own story from the mass of mementos in her Welsh family home – the unforgettably named Château Despair – she proves them devastatingly right.'
Vesna Goldsworthy, author of *Chernobyl Strawberries*

'This book was dangerous to write and is troubling to read. In courageously undertaking to chronicle the severe damage done to her gifted mind by early and prolonged emotional abuse Gwyneth Lewis risked psychological collapse. But while refusing to settle for a consoling narrative of complete recovery she succeeds in negotiating a liberating truce with her deeply troubled past. And so this remarkable volume ends in cautious optimism with the rebirth of a person and of a writer.'
M. Wynn Thomas, author of *Transatlantic Vistas*

NIGHTSHADE MOTHER

NIGHTSHADE MOTHER

A Disentangling

Gwyneth Lewis

2024

Reprinted 2024

www.uwp.co.uk

British Library Cataloguing-in-Publication Data

A catalogue record for this book is available from the British Library.

ISBN: 978-1-915279-90-3

Cover artwork by Jason Anscomb
Typeset by Agnes Graves
Printed and bound in Great Britain by Bell & Bain Ltd, Glasgow
The publisher acknowledges the financial support of the Books Council of Wales.

NIGHTSHADE (DEADLY)

(*Atropa Belladonna*)

This is the largest of the nightshades. It is five feet high, having several long spreading roots ... The flowers ... have a dismal aspect. They are large, hollow, and hang down like bells. On the outside they are of a dusky colour, between brown and green, and within they are purple. They are succeeded by berries of the size of cherries, black and shining when ripe, and full of a purplish juicy pulp, of a sweetish and mawkish taste.

This nightshade bears a very bad character as being of a poisonous nature. It is not good at all for inward uses.

(Culpeper)

They say that 'Time Assuages' –
Time never did assuage –
An actual suffering strengthens
As Sinews do, with Age –

(Emily Dickinson)

CONTENTS

Prelude

THE 'POWERS OF LOVE REVERSED'

> the matriarch and the changeling, looking
> at each other with a dismay that would seem
> like the powers of love reversed.
>
> (JOHN CHEEVER)

The last thing my mother said to me before she died was: 'Shut up!'

In hospital, suffering from pneumonia, Eryl began to call for her own parent: 'Mam.' Pause. 'Maam.' The plaintive moan was as penetrating as a lamb crying for her ewe. I overheard her comment to a nurse:

'I don't know why I want her, we didn't even get on.'

But, when it comes to the really big crises in life, only your mother will do.

While Eryl was unconscious but still alive, I asked her to forgive me for anything that I'd done wrong. I'm no saint. She could still hear, because she nodded. She never told me she loved me – that was too much to ask and, besides, Eryl's generation didn't speak like that to their children. I waited for an apology or, even, an acknowledgement, which would have changed everything, but it never came.

During one of the nights I kept vigil with her, Eryl began to show signs of agitation. Her hands made vague gestures in the air, as if she were struggling to locate her body. She tugged at the top button of her nightdress. Shakespeare's *King Lear*, which Eryl had taught many times, came to mind. At the lead's big moment in Act V, Scene 3, Lear enters carrying the corpse of his murdered daughter Cordelia and is told that his Fool has been killed. The actor needs full use of his vocal chords to do the tragedy justice. Then he utters the curious line: 'Pray you undo this button. Thank you, sir' before resuming his lament with the awful: 'O, o, o, o'. Critics think that these words are an ad lib, transcribed in error. His costume is choking him and so he asks a fellow performer to help him. I checked Mam's button, but it was fine and she could speak if she wanted to.

I didn't dare hold Eryl's hand, even though she was dying. Soon she became more restless, so I called a nurse. Welsh speakers can identify each other even when conversing in English so, while she was preparing an injection, the nurse and I made small talk in *Cymraeg*, our voices low ('an excellent thing in a woman', according to Lear). Suddenly, Eryl commanded:

'Shut up!'

Even at death's door, she couldn't bear for me to speak.

I missed Eryl's last breath but I sat for a while with the body.

Out loud, I said:

'Well, we had a good fight.'

Already I felt safer.

> 'I think my mother's death is the best thing to happen to me since … well, since my father's death,' said Patrick.
>
> (Edward St Aubyn)

There's an old farming saying relating to the practice of placing weak chicks in the hearth to survive: '*Y cyw a fegir yn uffern, yn uffern y myn fod*' ('The chick that's reared in hell, will insist on staying in hell'). The proverb plays on the double meaning of the word 'uffern', which is derived from the Latin 'inferno' but also refers to the ash-pit near an open fire, a warm place for weak creatures to be given a chance to thrive. Deprived of its mother, a chick or lamb will stick to the refuge it knows and identify even the mouth of hell as its saviour.

I doubt if a handful of people know the full story of what I'm about to describe or understand how crippled I've been by Eryl's emotional abuse of me. I look like a competent person – sober over thirty years, working at an art that I love, unexpectedly married to Leighton for decades. And yet, I still experience catastrophic

Eryl and Gwilym Lewis's wedding

collapses in my confidence which leave me gasping for breath and feeling suicidal. I don't seem to know my own mind, or to recognise what being on my own side might be. The damage has nearly killed me – not once or twice, but multiple times.

I'm down in Cardiganshire, staying near where my great-grandfather farmed, when the equinoctial gales arrive. It's raining heavily and the drops in puddles make round eyes, which look at me reproachfully. My retired racing greyhound, Jen, runs in her sleep. The weather clears and we sit outside. The dog pricks up her ears. We hear a hunting bugle and a pack of hounds in the next valley moving towards us, then three very loud gunshots. I put Jen's harness and coat on her, and we head down to the river.

A hulking man stands on the bridge, resting a twelve-bore on the stone parapet. He's obviously there to head off the fox. I ask him in English what's happening. As he answers, we switch into Welsh. I mentioned where I'm from, as Welsh speakers do – the equivalent of dogs sniffing each other's rears. In exchange, he blurts out his name and village but immediately covers his tracks, twitchy about whether I will report what is clearly an illegal hunt (I don't). Jen provides a talking point, as my pal has kept greyhounds for hare coursing. He begins to relax:

'Have you got a husband?'

Just then I see something red coming through the larches on the slope facing us.

'Fox!'

'No, hounds,' he said. 'They had the fox earlier.'

Jen wants to join in and we agree that she'd beat the pack, at least for a while. The man says he's going to move on down towards the sea. I ask if it's safe to follow.

'I'd prefer it if you went that way,' he said, pointing in the opposite direction.

'Then I'll take your advice.'

Jen and I turn uphill towards the village. Further on, I meet a woman outside her house. She's wearing full make-up and is furious, clutching a phone in her hand.

'Bastard! He shouldn't have a gun anywhere near a public highway.'

She's already called the police.

With a jolt, I'm back in the world of judgement. Until then, I've been too interested in seeing what's happening, without condemning it, to even think about which 'side' I should take, though I know the relevant welfare, cultural and political arguments. I've been observing, as any writer does. Don't waste time moralising (that can come later, if ever), just notice as much as you can, and listen.

It's only when I'm back in the house that I begin to feel the shame. Shame at being unable to take an immediate stance on the hunt, as others do; that I dare to be in a place I love on such a beautiful day (that's not allowed!); that I've been writing that morning (what an act of treachery!). I sit on the floor next to the dog, sobbing and rocking back and forth. This is what maternal emotional abuse does: it shuts you out of your own resources. And the effect becomes stronger with time. My mind perceives me as a trespasser in my own life, to be repelled using scorn. Emotionally, I'm booby-trapped.

This is how people kill themselves, in ferocious and unexpected pain, just when they'd begun to trust that, perhaps, at last, things might be going well. You've only to add some alcohol or drug abuse, and it becomes impossible to ride the wave of distress. Next thing and you're a two-inch paragraph in the local newspaper. I've come to recognise this precipitous decline in mood as part of my inheritance from growing up in my strange, dysfunctional family. It is one of my mother's kisses.

Gwilym and Eryl Lewis, my parents, both migrated from Welsh hinterlands of Ogmore Vale and Cardiganshire respectively in the 1950s to look for work in Cardiff. They met at a club for Welsh speakers called Tŷ'r Cymry ('House of the Welsh'), as if they were in a foreign country, rather than in the capital city of their own. My father noticed that my mother was wearing red boots; she heard him being told to stop being a tease. Next thing, there are photos of their wedding in December 1956, in the porch of Capel y Crwys in Cathays.

'It's all a bit quick,' commented my father's sister Enid when they told her. She made a bad impression on Eryl because she was wearing nail varnish and smoking a cigarette, which my mother considered 'common'. Eryl never forgave her the false insinuation that they had to get married.

Our photograph album is a loose-leaf volume of black pages, tied in between embossed leather covers. There's only the one book, which ends in about 1973, as if our life as a family fizzled out after that. Photos had to be inserted into adhesive corners, and occasions labelled in white paint, like Tippex. Looking at my parents' wedding pictures, I'm struck by the strong grip Gwilym has taken of Eryl's palm. She has removed her gloves and clutches them: one couple, six hands, an emblem of the dowry she'd brought from her own difficult upbringing. In a few years, she'll pass that parcel on to me.

If you'd asked me, I'd have told you that I'd forgiven my parents and was loving them as best I could, but you can't forgive someone until you know the full cost to you of what that person's done. As an adult, I was mature enough to know that my parents no longer had authority over me and couldn't tell me what to do. I stopped fighting with them and limited what I told them about my life. Continued contact meant that I could never lapse into fantasies about them (as I would have, had I withdrawn). They remained part of my life, I knew them as they were. I wanted such love as there was to be had. Besides, Welsh-speaking girls are meant to be dutiful daughters.

My sister and I looked after our ageing parents as best we could. We visited regularly then, did their shopping, took them to medical appointments and hospitals. I had Power of Attorney over their financial matters. Leighton and I happened to live two minutes down the road and, so, could be there quickly if anybody fell over. Gwilym died in 2013, two and a half years before Eryl did the same.

I cared for them gladly but being a good daughter was part of my ultimate exit strategy. It was important to me to do the right thing by them so that I had no grounds for self-reproach. The rage came later and, in its wake, a de-forgiving.

> Every household god becomes a monument and every room a grave.
>
> (Charles Dickens)

Clearing my parents' house after they died is the worst task I've ever done. Brought up just before the Second World War, rationing and austerity had made them hoarders. Gwilym's garage was a storehouse of things that 'might come in handy': jam-jars were kept and filled with elastic bands thrown down by the postman, stray nails and miscellaneous screws. One plastic bag held five door locks and handles. Eryl held on to every box of colouring crayons that had ever come her way, including those she used as a child in the 1930s. In one tin, we found chalk stubs from her teaching days; in another, several single dolls' shoes.

Gwilym kept all instruction manuals, even for appliances which had been replaced, including a brochure for double glazing two sets of windows ago. At the end of his life, he'd clip weather forecasts out of the newspaper and stow them in one of his shoes. There were pamphlets describing every castle or museum we'd visited on day trips as a family, as if information about these destinations were in danger of disappearing. The wall calendars on which doctors' appointments were written were all kept, like footprints from day to day, evidence in a court case. Mam retained every single receipt for grocery shopping clipped into an accounts book and decades of cheque stubs were collected in a brown leather case stashed under my parents' double bed.

This had left the Lewis household with an archive which reminds me of a cache of Jewish holy writings, known as a *geniza*. Because the word of God is holy, traditionally, no scrap of writing relating to a synagogue was destroyed. Out-of-date paperwork was collected in a separate room, providing a random picture of the community's quotidian business. This practice has meant that over a thousand years' worth of manuscripts has been kept, for example, in the Ben Ezra Synagogue in Cairo, from 870 CE to the nineteenth century. I'm not suggesting that these trivia from our house are holy but, amassed together, they form a picture of several generations of one family's life. My delight in these scraps – not important in themselves – is also part of my artistic interest in the ordinary, rather than the exceptional. A cousin recently visited my great-grandfather's farm as its owner (another cousin) had just died. From the *cwtsh-dan-stâr* (the cubby under the stairs) he retrieved a wire onto which were threaded dozens of invoices paid to blacksmiths, farriers, clog-makers and other tradesmen, a fascinating archive of farm expenditure.

I've inherited this inability to throw any piece of paper that comes through my hands, placing letters and cards in boxes. I still retain some notes that my friends and I used to pass to each other when we were bored in school, our teenage writing minuscule. As we were clearing drawers in the house, my sister and I even folded the newspapers that lined them – some from the 1960s – 'Just in case there's something of interest'. There wasn't.

Eryl kept every fountain pen the family had ever used. This discovery thrilled me, as I'm writing this with a black Cross with a converter and fine nib. Years before, I'd asked if I could have the vintage pens with green stripes and art deco blues but Eryl refused, even though they were being kept in a drawer. I tackled the decades of encrusted ink by soaking the pens in a glass dish, bleeding streamers of red, blue and black. When I tried them out, not one of the pens worked. Why keep and leave broken instruments, as if they were heirlooms? The self I inherited from my parents is similarly dysfunctional, no use to me in the present, however essential in the past.

As we were clearing Gwilym and Eryl's home, Leighton suggested that, instead of selling it, he and I should renovate and go to live there.

In 1972, when I was twelve, my parents had moved to a big 1950s house with panoramic views of Cardiff from Somerset in the south to the opening of the south Wales valleys in the north. By the time Leighton and I were married, we called the house Château Despair or Ice Station Zebra because, if you opened the front door for too long, you let out the cold. Everything in it smelt – not of dirt, but of dog, books and lives grown static. My parents had a window cleaner who did the windows facing the street, but they didn't see the point in paying him for the back, with its inspiring views. They shut the curtains against the light. Dust accumulated and Eryl didn't welcome visitors, in case they criticised her housekeeping.

I wanted to sell the house.

'Don't let a dead woman win,' said Leighton.

I agreed to try living there, on condition that we move if I couldn't cope.

Leighton and I disagree about almost everything, but I've learned to listen to his instincts. He's right more often than I care to admit. He pointed out that it made financial sense for us to move in. After all, the building itself wasn't the issue, but my attitude to it, which could be changed. We could make the place our own. Leighton's optimism wore me down until, despite my misgivings, I agreed to the plan. We'd been looking for a new place to live for a couple of years and hadn't seen anything better. The best way to get rid of an eyesore in your view is to go to live in it. I felt exhilarated by the prospect of coming home on my own terms.

William Faulkner has the best description I know of how a house plays its own history on its inhabitants' bodies. Climbing the stairs of a former dwelling, Miss Rosa notices that:

> an echo spoke which was not mine but rather that of the lost irrevocable might-have-been which haunts all houses, all enclosed walls erected by human hands, not for shelter, not for warmth, but to hide from the world's curious looking and seeing the dark turnings which the ancient young delusions of pride and hope and ambition (ay, and love too) take.

The physical memories were strong. I knew exactly the noise rainwater makes in the drainpipe outside the upstairs toilet when the wind is from the north-west, how the TV aerial on the roof judders when a perching bird launches from it. The second step of the stair still creaked, so my left foot automatically still went to the third, from the habit of trying to move around the house without waking my parents.

We had builders knock through walls to create a long living room at the sunny back of the house. A kitchen was put in the former sitting room. We made a new space by combining the upstairs toilet and bathroom to make me a study. Leighton planted grapevines, honeysuckle and clematis and trained them over a new pergola. Château Despair is now a hospitable, generous house; not the mean, fearful place it used to be. When I show people the view from our bedroom, visitors exclaim with surprise and delight.

The day we moved in, a robin entered the front door ahead of us, hopped through the house, leaving by the new patio doors. We'd often joked that my father looked like a robin because he liked red shirts and had skinny legs. At the time, it felt like a blessing.

There's more to inheritance than any financial estate left by the deceased. Both my parents were migraineurs, so I'm the beneficiary of a genetic double whammy. My first migraine attack happened when I was ten years old and they've been with me, like increasingly malevolent ghosts, ever since.

Over the years, the migraines changed from occasional events and became regular, generally related to my menstrual cycle. Gradually they spilt over into the rest of the month, happening ever more frequently. I tried to avoid the usual trigger foods – chocolate, cheese, oranges and caffeine being the most obvious – but the number of headaches continued to increase. I say 'headache', but migraine is a faulty brainwave that disrupts multiple physical functions. I know I have one approaching when I feel a stab of pain in one eye. I often – but not always – see a flash or aura. Light and noise are cranked up to rave levels. Once the infallible sign of sinusitis pain down the side of my nose appears, there's nothing to be done but to take medication and sleep it off in a darkened room. The migraineur is said to have an 'over-excitable brain'. Sensory stimuli that don't bother others make us ill. I can't bear the smell of lilies.

I've been known to move from a good seat at a concert because another woman's perfume is making me want to throw up.

I hit the clinical definition of chronic, as opposed to episodic, migraine a decade and a half ago. This means suffering fifteen or more headache days a month. Migraine is more common than diabetes, asthma and epilepsy combined. The World Health Organization considers chronic migraine to be among the most disabling disorders, comparable in gravity to psychosis, dementia and quadriplegia.[1]

During this period of moving into my parents' old house, I had been going to America to teach, which had been a lifelong ambition. Even though I was doing work I loved, the attacks continued to increase in frequency and severity. Now I was migrainous nearly every day and could do nothing but teach and go straight back to bed. I'd become so cold that I'd have to take a hot shower, clutch a hot water bottle and wear a woolly hat when outside temperatures were in the nineties. In a while, I'd feel a white-hot dagger of pain being thrust through one eyeball, down the side of my nose and out through the back of my skull. For brief periods, I couldn't see, speak or understand what was being said to me. Light and noise were unbearable and I'd become confused. From being a highly organised person, my paperwork was in chaos and I made errors that baffled me. I blamed myself for failing to achieve a healthy work/life balance and tried to be more resilient.

Three years after Leighton and I moved into our new home, I became totally incapacitated by migraines. Social life had stopped and writing couldn't happen, let alone paid work. Pain silenced me, but the shocking decline in my mental abilities was for me by far the worst aspect of the disorder. My words became mixed up. For example, I'd see a rainbow, but would call it a library. I'd tell Leighton that I was going to put the washing out in the oven to dry. My words were shuffled in my brain, like a deck of cards. I

---

1 'The State of the Migraine Nation', *Migraine Trust*, *https://migrainetrust.org/wp-content/uploads/2021/08/State-of-the-Migraine-Nation-population-rapid-review.pdf.*

couldn't read, watch a programme or answer e-mails. I found myself completely stalled in everything that I cared about.

Chronic pain began to wear down my defences against Château Despair and I started to feel like a double-exposed film. Increasingly, I saw the house with twin vision, with our new, happier layout superimposed over the former plan. Now, when I was stupid with brain fog, I found myself walking to pee where the bathroom used to be – now rebuilt into a study. I was unable to defend myself from the deep physical memories being in the house evoked. They flashed across my mind, like migraine auras, preventing me from seeing the present. Entering the garage would conjure up my father wearing my old school duffle coat, in his 'smoking room' sitting in a deck chair, tending to his pipe, a galvanised bucket next to him for the dottle. Picking up the coal scuttle in order to bank up the fire, I'd recall a photo of me as a spotty teenager in the same corner, where my parents put the Christmas tree: me in an M&S quilted nylon dressing gown, pointing to a tin of processed peas someone had given me as a joke. These images were like electric shocks, as if the house were dangerously wired, without an earth. I was living in two houses at once. No wonder I was feeling sick on land, and unable to think straight. I was so debilitated that I became convinced that my dead parents' old age had, like a spirit, taken possession of my body. Against my will, I was living as they did: turning away from the world, medicating emotional distress and pain with almost full-time sleep. I felt as though I was in my eighties, waiting for the end.

For me, the most problematic room was the main bedroom, where my parents had slept. Later, it became my mother's room. It was in the shady front of the house and I hated it. In an attempt to repurpose it, the architect suggested that we turn it into a library. My parents were great readers and kept books in every single room of the house. At one time, there were piles on the staircase, which made rapid descent dangerous. The books were of no antiquarian value but had been well used. I kept my grandfather's sets of complete Dickens and H. G. Wells, which had been purchased by subscription from newspapers. My mother or her sister had scribbled all over the 1936 *Rupert Bear Annual*, so it was of no interest to collectors. Even when

I'd weeded out old school textbooks, novels I'd read and didn't want to revisit, there must have been six thousand volumes left, to which I added over five thousand of my own. The sheer materiality of so many words weighed heavily on me.

We reinforced the floor of the dark room and commissioned a carpenter to make shelving. There would be no need to go in there, except to fetch a book and take it to my new study at the sunny back of the house. Only I was too afraid to enter. Years after moving in, my swanky new 'library' was still full of unsorted books in chaos. I imagined life as a party going on elsewhere: Bunyan was in conversation with Dostoevsky, H.D. whispering to Czesław Miłosz. Marina Tsvetaeva quizzing an old Baedeker of Switzerland; Stevie Smith smoked in the corner, leafing through a Welsh hymn book. I couldn't find a thing. I kept the door closed, the locked room in Bluebeard's castle. It was as if I'd placed my mind at my mother's mercy.

One morning, I woke to feel the familiar knife in the eye, for the twenty-sixth day that month. I experienced abdominal migraine – new to me – so severe that I thought I'd pass out with the pain. Somewhere, I could hear moaning. When the screaming started, I realised that it was me.

Another migraine lasted six weeks with no respite. The doctors told me to limit painkiller use, which I did. When all else failed, walking helped with the trigeminal pain, nausea and disorientation. But I couldn't spend my life walking the streets of Cardiff in a daze. I left a message for my neurologist that I was in *status migrainosus* and suicidal but never heard back from him.

I could no longer be relied on to walk the dog. Luckily I had a greyhound, a breed that needs little exercise and is capable of sleeping for most of the day. When I could go out with the dog, I'd taken to wandering through Cathays cemetery, the sprawling Victorian and Edwardian burial ground built in 1859. There were few people and many squirrels for Jen's entertainment (she never caught any) and I enjoyed reading the monumental gravestones of Cardiff's civic dead, from archbishops to shipping magnates, victims of the Cardiff Blitz, boxing legend Jim Driscoll to 14-year-old Louisa Maud Evans, who fell from a hot-air balloon over the Bristol Channel. Mysteriously, none of the graves seemed to stay put. Once I'd found them, they seemed to circulate according to their own rules and would prove impossible to find again, like the irretrievable books in my library.

Two walks in the cemetery stand out. Shortly after Christmas I passed a woman my age placing fresh flowers on a grave. I commented how nice it was to see that they were fresh and not plastic and the woman said to me: 'Thirty years they've been dead and I still miss them'. I had a sudden sense of the warmth and affection possible in relation to parents. I didn't miss mine at all. My experience of them had been more like handling dangerous knives. My face must have looked stricken because the woman stepped towards me and asked if I was all right. I sobbed that no, I wasn't, but social distancing and my own pain meant that I repelled her proffered hug. If I started crying, I felt that I'd never stop. My grief made me experience the trauma of my upbringing with full force for the first time. I'd been warding off the blows for years and now, with the added burden of chronic migraine, I could no longer bear them. Perhaps it was now safe enough to feel it all.

The second walk puzzled the dog. I was ill again and so desperate that I wanted to impale my left eye on one of the wrought-iron railings surrounding the cemetery. Luckily, I'd remembered to bring my phone. Leighton, I felt, was already distressed enough by my suffering, so I phoned a friend who knew exactly what to say. I hid among the graves until I'd calmed down, while the dog, in her red coat, wandered here and there among the tombs, doubling back from time to time to check on me.

Chronic migraine is not a psychosomatic illness, but research has shown that suffering an adverse childhood experience makes you 12 per cent more likely to suffer and 40 per cent more likely if the abuse is emotional.[2] The emotional tenor of the physical gestures

2 Gretchen Tietjen, 'Link Between Unresolved Trauma and Migraine', *Migraine World Summit*, *https://migraineworldsummit.com/talk/link-between-unresolved-trauma-and-migraine/*.

occasioned by the disorder didn't escape me. Here I was, spending days in bed, covering my eyes with both hands, hiding in the dark, the universal gesture of shame. Even with the blind down, my head under the duvet, wearing an eye mask, the palms of my hands over my eyes, eyelids pressed shut, there was still too much light for my brain to bear. What if I was trying to hide from what the house was telling me, like the incestuous Oedipus, blinding himself with his mother's brooches?

One day, facing the same dazzle of pain and with no prospect of defending myself against it, I decided to kill myself. I had no idea how to do it but thought that, if I had a drink, something suitably chaotic would happen and I'd work it out. Luckily, I knew how to distract myself from the suggestions of my old enemy, alcohol, as I've had thirty-plus years' experience doing so. But it was too close for comfort. How had things come to this?

Writing a book about an abusive parent requires meticulous good faith and a proper degree of fear. When they were alive, I never called my parents by their first names. In fact, I wasn't even allowed to address them by the familiar '*ti*' in Welsh; even more oddly, they used the formal '*chi*' (like '*vous*' in French) towards each other. In this book I use their first names because I'm now their equal and want to consider them as people apart from my family relationship to them. Impossible, but I'll try. The childish part of me has never lost her fear of my 'olders and betters'.

When Sherman Alexie, the Navajo author, was promoting his book, *You Don't Have to Say You Love Me*, about his mother, he cancelled the tour, because he became convinced that her reproachful ghost was haunting him. Given that my life with Eryl is literally imprinted on my blood chemistry, she's an ever-present artefact in my body. Her death has done nothing to disperse that effect. In describing my experience of emotional abuse at her hands, I risk arousing a crisis of auto-immunity. What I'm about to write would be, in Eryl's eyes, a gross betrayal, the worst thing I could possibly do to her.

While she was alive, Eryl possessed an almost psychic ability to detect when I was withholding information. Then a horrible thought occurred to me. What if, in the afterlife, she'd become omniscient? What if now she could see everything I was doing and, somewhere offstage, was brewing storms of rage and disapproval, magnified by her new divine abilities? What if she were generating a cosmic revenge on me? I've already had a dream that Eryl turned up at the launch of this book. 'How am I going to make this all right for her?' was my first, terrified thought.

Given how grave the trespass of outing a narcissist is, I need to know when the bladed wheel is going to swing towards me as I raid the ancestors' tomb. I certainly don't want to deploy my own weapons against myself. The task in front of me is as delicate as pulling a fishhook embedded in my eye.

Being brought up in a minority community further inhibits frankness. Because gossip is so rampant, secrets are buried all the deeper. Anything that tarnishes the image of the group in its own mind and in front of the majority is doubly denied. Eryl taught English in high school and I regularly meet former pupils who declare her to be the best teacher they ever had. This is true: she was outstanding and highly respected. Recently, I was sitting with a schoolfriend on a beach. She'd been one of Eryl's pupils while we were both in school. We looked out at a calm sea and she said:

'Your mother was so lovely.'

I said nothing. I didn't know whether to feel virtuous for being loyal to Eryl, or a heel for being false to myself and my friend.

Aesthetics are at the core of the relationship between my mother and me. Perhaps the most puzzling aspect of my reaction to the emotional abuse I suffered was how I returned to its poison, like an addict or the chick returning to its hell. No matter how shattering a recent visit to Mam would prove, I'd eventually forget and go back for more. This amnesia reminds me of Coleridge's formulation of an audience's 'willing suspension of disbelief' in theatre. What kept me captive to a toxic performance art was that I simply wasn't convinced that a person – my own mother – could be so mean. I didn't believe in her character. My distress at not receiving the emotional support I needed was proof that I had some concept of a benign mother. But she was the only one I'd ever known, so why would I think that anything could ever be different? What was the source of this other idea? Could it be that we all have a physical conception of a mother archetype deep in our bodies, so that we know that aberrant behaviour isn't right?

As an adult, I learned never, ever to trust Eryl. Occasionally, though, I would forget this golden rule due to exhaustion or being distracted. One day, I admitted that I was feeling low because a commission that had been extremely demanding didn't feel as though it had paid off. Quick as a whip, Eryl responded:

'Why were you such a fool as to put so much time and effort into something so uncertain?'

The blow landed with the force of a Triffid's ten-foot stinger in the heart. I was speechless. I could have said: Because that's what it takes for me to be a writer. I risk everything every time, otherwise, there's no life in the work. And you've just wiped out what I am. Instead, I picked up my things and left, calling myself a fool for letting my guard down.

Eryl had wanted to be a writer herself, so I suppose that my complaining about my work hit a raw nerve. The difference between a writer who doesn't practise the art and one who does is exactly this willingness to wander in and out of folly. I should have answered that there's no greater fool than the person who refuses to be one.

Welsh-language nationalism centres on the metaphor of the endangered mother tongue, which has to be saved, at all costs. Metaphorically, therefore, all Welsh speakers are children whose interests are less important than their progenitor. But language never gave birth to anybody. It's more like a lens that focuses the eye in particular political and existential directions. There is a danger that this is culturally infantilising, putting loyalty before the exercise of free will. I'm passionate about language preservation but deeply wounded by the mother who taught me Welsh. This is not to devalue the language, but to point to nuances in my attitude to it as part of my inheritance. Maryse Condé, the novelist from Guadeloupe, offers a liberating insight: 'For a writer, there is no mother tongue: he forges his own language according to his or her needs.'[3]

Part of the damage done to me is that I'm programmed to put Eryl's version of events before my own. What I'm doubting, of course, is my own veracity. In this book the evidence is really important to me. I quote from my parents' diaries and the journals that I kept off and on since I was seven years old. I need this material for two reasons. The first is that, having been gaslit since childhood, I'm still deeply distrustful of my own version of events and need corroboration. The second is that I'm determined not to treat anybody, including Eryl, the way she dealt with me: irrationally and unfairly. This is the most important freedom I have from this toxic experience and, for all my justified anger, is the most potent antidote in my moral medicine cabinet.

Eryl enjoyed playing the piano and did so late into her life. I picked the soundtrack for her funeral from among the sheet music that I found propped on the stand. There was a brief time while I, aged about eleven, was learning to play the instrument, when Eryl would play duets with me. She took the more difficult bass part, while I banged out the treble melody. This is my happiest memory of us together. Eryl soon became irritated by my demands that we play these pieces repeatedly. Soon, I was back to the loneliness of practising scales and set pieces for the Royal Schools of Music exams. The memory of us sitting arm-to-arm on the piano stool, our four hands making a larger sound than we could manage individually, is a tantalising glimpse of how much Eryl and I might have enjoyed each other.

However, at about the same age, I remember standing in front of the same piano and confiding to my mother that I loved the new

---

3 'A Q&A with Maryse Condé', *London Review of Books* blog, August 2020, *https://www.londonreviewbookshop.co.uk/blog/2020/november/for-a-writer-there-is-no-mother-tongue-he-forges-his-own-language-according-to-his-or-her-needs-a-q-a-with-maryse-conde*.

best friend I'd made in school. She mocked me for that, repeating my secret in a withering tone, which hurt me deeply. Why would loving somebody ever be a problem? In a moment of remorse afterwards, she told me that she was only trying to 'harden' me, for my own good. No. She was being cruel, and I still have no idea why.

> You always took the darkest view of anything connected with me. Sometimes you knew best. But more often you were mistaken … It seems to me now that perhaps you needed a villain in the family, and that villain was me.
>
> (Georges Simenon)

In the very last stages of Eryl's dying, I left the hospital to come home for a shower. I was about to rest when, knowing that time was running out, I was seized by a desire to see my mother while I still could. She was a monster, but she was *my* monster.

As for now, I don't know if I'm more afraid of finding how much I hate my mother or, despite everything, how much I love her.

—You've forgotten about me.

—Who's that?

—Old friend.

—You sound familiar.

—I'm not relative, if that's what you mean. I was always imagined.

—Can I trust you?

—That's for you to find out. I'll tell you one thing, though, I'll never, ever, tell you to shut up.

Author's Note

I have quoted diary entries and letters verbatim, without correcting the grammar or mutations. Welsh is not as standardised as English and here I value the sense of how the writer speaks and feels over orthographical purity. I have added some letters in square brackets, however, in order to help with legibility. The usual spelling of 'Mam-gu' is with a hyphen, but I've stuck to the family way of omitting it.

TOXINS

But I beseech your grace, without offence,
(My conscience bids me ask) wherefore you have
Commanded of me these most poisonous compounds,
Which are the movers of a languishing death:
But though slow, deadly.

(Shakespeare, *Cymbeline*)

Chapter 1
INVALID

The only heirloom that I ever wanted from my parents' house was the Crugeryr grandfather clock. My sister could have anything else: the oak linen press, the chest of drawers with diamond-shaped ivory inlays made by our paternal great-grandfather. It stands now in the hall, stitching the day with its ticking.

The timepiece is a tough, rural piece of furniture. The date 1783 is carved into the mechanism, so this clock was working before the French Revolution or the battles of Trafalgar and Waterloo. Under the XII on the face is the name of D. Jones and, below it, Llandysul, where it was made. In the semi-circle at the apex of the face is a strange river scene, showing a cottage, mountains in the distance, and cows up to their knees in water, drinking – a pastoral vision of a no-place, nothing like rural west Wales.

It looks as though the painted Roman numerals from VII onwards are smudged but the injury goes deeper: the hands have gouged tracks in the face's enamel. In this clock, the passage of time isn't gentle. Chronology is always, in the end, violent. In order to avoid being challenged by his children, the old god Chronos bit off the heads of his offspring. The clock's mechanism is simple and resembles a bicycle and chain. Chiming on each hour, the bell sounds like the 'Seconds Out!' signal in a boxing ring. At its base, the case's planks have parted, and sections of the inlay set into its body are missing. Until Leighton removed them, there were dabs of paint on its feet, though I would have been quite happy for these marks of use to remain.

The Crugeryr clock chimes on the hour, day and night. Lying awake, unable to sleep, after languishing in bed with constant migraine, it places my life in the broader soundscape of generations of our family. This means dealing with the unwelcome rhymes in experience between generations.

The chronically ill live in Annwn, a Celtic Otherworld. It's a parallel time created by genetics and lived experience. Resting does nothing to heal this condition, because its inhabitants have been kidnapped and can't find their way home. Instead of moving forward in chronology, we regress, sometimes to the experiences of previous generations.

The clock chimes once. I used to be out in the world, could run for an hour on a trail; I wrote books, had a social life and a laugh. Now I'm a maggot tucked into a shroud. Two a.m. strikes. Eryl spent much of her time in bed, brought down by ill health and depression. Three o'clock. My grandmother, Sarah Ann (Mamgu), was bedridden for much of her life.

—Are you being an invalid out of loyalty to foremothers?
—How dare you! Nobody wants to be ill.

Blinded by migraine, I've forgotten the concerns of humans who are up and about, dealing with each other, talking. Even the light hurts. I feel blotted out, no longer viable, totally invalid.

Were we, all three – Sarah Ann, Eryl and me – laid low by the same poison?

I can trace the dark, toxic thread in our family back to Crugeryr (spellings vary), where my grandmother, Sarah Ann Jones, was born in 1894. The Joneses' ancestors had lived in Crugeryr Isaf in Talgarreg village, Ceredigion (Cardiganshire), since the dissolution of the monasteries. They were part of the large Herbert family who'd risen from cattle rustlers to aristocracy in the Tudor Age. The poet George Herbert and I share a great-grandfather eleven generations ago.

My grandmother's older sister – Magdalen Jane – was named after Magdalen Herbert, the poet's mother. Born in 1893 she lived for only a year. Eryl's ferocious mother, Sarah Ann, was born the year after her sister died and became the eldest of five surviving girls and one boy. Eryl herself didn't like staying in Crugeryr as a child, because household members peed outside the back door, which she thought uncouth.

Some years ago, I was visiting Soar y Mynydd (the 'Mountain Soar'), the tiny Methodist chapel in the Cambrian Mountains above Llanddewi Brefi, one of the rare places where perfect silence could, at that time, be heard. I fell into conversation with two local women wearing floral crimplene dresses in patterns that Stanley Spencer called 'rich earth' when describing such figures in his Cookham cemetery paintings.

As people do in a small country, the ladies wormed my family connections with the area out of me. They remembered my grandmother. After a pause, they agreed with each other:

'*Roedd hi'n fenyw gryf.*'

('She was a strong woman.')

I knew exactly what they meant but weren't saying.

The Crugeryr daughters were known to be 'characterful'. Olwen kept a pub in London and another sister caused a nonconformist scandal when she was rumoured to have had an affair with the village schoolmaster and to have born his child out of wedlock. During the Second World War, the Joneses employed Nikko, a Ukrainian prisoner of war, who simply stayed on after peace was declared and became part of the community.

I was once passing a building site in Aberaeron and was stopped in my tracks to see the name Crug-Yr-Eryr printed on the side of a sack of gravel. Above the farm is a quarry of the same name which operates bilingually. It pleases me that shingle from a quarry on the same ridge is now incorporated into the structure of new buildings and old walls all over Ceredigion. The emotional aggregate of that particular rise has shaped the home in which I was brought up and the nerve-endings in my own ruined sense of self.

My mother's name, 'Eryl', is, clearly, a reference to Crugeryr Isaf. I'd assumed that the 'eryr' part of the name referred to an eagle. Eryri, which is the Welsh name for Snowdonia, is often thought to denote the same raptor and, by extension, the princes for whom it became a metaphor. The word actually means 'land rise'. *Eryr* is also the Welsh name for shingles, because the raised blisters of that viral infection are like knolls in a landscape. Crugeryr Isaf, therefore, is a tautology, meaning Lower Top of the Hill, as opposed to Crugeryr Uchaf – Upper Top of the Hill – just up the slope. This fine distinction reminds me of a characteristically Welsh joke about a man boarding a bus in Cwmsgwt and asking for a one-way ticket to Mumbai. The driver issued the ticket and, after a few months of wandering the Indian subcontinent, the traveller entered the Mumbai bus station. At the kiosk, he asked for a one-way ticket to Cwmsgwt. The clerk then enquired:

'Upper or Lower?'

It surprises me now that, although Crugeryr Isaf was a minute away from my great-aunt's house, we were never taken to see the farm, even from the road. The first time I saw the place was just after the Covid pandemic, when it was for sale. I phoned the owner – who had a Birmingham accent – to explain that it had been in the family and would he give me permission to look round? He refused, but I went to look at the outside anyway. The outbuildings had been converted to house visitors. The grounds were neglected and the whole place had a depressing air. Soon after, the place was sold and the new owners caused a stir by translating the name into English, an affront to Welsh speakers in the area, who often refer to people not by surname but by Christian name, combined with their house or farm. We knew Marged Jane as 'Anti Eryri', her address. The new owners wisely kept the name and you can now go to stay at Crug Yr Eryr Isaf in beautifully refurbished cottages. It's not a place that I feel compelled to revisit.

I don't know where my grandfather, Ben James, and my grandmother, Sarah Ann Jones, met but barely ten miles divide Llwyndafydd, his village, from her Talgarreg. Their courtship took place in the shadow of the First World War. Ben James enlisted with the Royal Welch Fusiliers in 1915 and, initially, was a musketry and physical therapy instructor, later transferring to the Royal Engineers' Gas Corps as a corporal. Later in the war, on 3 August 1918, he noted in his diary that he'd submitted his name for commission in infantry but, later, he's told by his superior that his case is 'hopeless'. This was because there was a glut of non-commissioned officers in the company. During the Second World War, when Ben James was a highly respected village school headmaster, he was made commander of Number 2 Platoon of the Home Guard at Llanddewi Brefi, organised the local Air Raid Prevention Services and was billeting officer for evacuees from Liverpool, London and East Grinstead. One report from a superior complemented the section on the high standard of proficiency in grenade throwing. Back in First World War Belgium, Ben James was wounded and sent to Fontainebleau and then to Saffron Waldon to recover. I have photographs of him smoking with his fellow soldiers, wearing the blue uniform of the convalescent. The cigarette smoke is a smudge, as if it were moving at a much faster pace than the posed men, or as if Ben James had breathed out a ghost. He has his hand, I notice, on the shoulder of a very attractive nurse seated in front of him. After recovering, he was then sent back to the front and took part in some of the bloodiest battles of the First World War. He was certainly present at the Fifth Battle of Ypres between September and October 1918.

Ben James's *Allies' Diary* for 1918 was a present from Sarah Ann Jones, who'd written 'Wishing you a Happy New Year' on the flyleaf and her address at Crugeryr Isaf with a note 'Please Forward To' – presumably in case the object of her affection be killed. The couple's initials are surrounded by a heart drawn with emphasis by my grandfather, Dacu. Ben wrote his own address underneath hers: Penarfawr, Cross Inn, Cardiganshire, south Wales where Owen James, his father, was a tenant farmer. It was a big deal, therefore, when, in 1928, he was able to buy land to build his own house. He broadcast his achievement in the name: Brynowen, 'Owen's Hill' – or 'Look what I did! – and it remained in the family until very recently.

The understated entries in the 1918 diary and letters home play down the horror of what Ben James must have experienced at the front: 'we had a warm reception from Fritz'. But events are not all grim. On Sunday, 31 March 1918, there's 'a party in the Hall singing before us. Sound very beautiful.' On 3 August 1918, Ben James notes that he's 'afraid of a hostile attack coming off.' Meanwhile, he's 'manning battle trenches' and 'rolling wire'. On Sunday, 4 August, a corporal of the military police takes his name 'for not screening window @ 10.13'. The action becomes lively towards the end of the war, with Ben noting on Friday, 27 September 1918: 'Fritz shelling with heavy guns at intervals during the night.'

The 1918 diary and postcards from the front interest me most for the evidence that they give about my grandparents' relationship. On Sunday, 24 February 1918, Ben's thinking of love in Welsh:

Blodau'r flwyddyn yw f'anwylyd
Ebrill, Mai, Mehefin hefyd.
Ma'i fel haul'n tywynu ar gyscod …

(My love is the flowers of the year
April, May and also June.
She's like sun that shines on shadow ...)

His passion is suggested by verses Ben quotes from a Samuel Taylor Coleridge poem, 'Love'. First published as 'Introduction to the Tale of the Dark Ladie', the ballad tells how a minstrel falls in love with Genevieve and woos her with the story of a knight defeating a monster. For 'Genevieve', read 'Sarah Ann':

She wept with pity & delight,
She blushed with love, & virgin shame,
And like the murmur of a dream,
I heard her breathe my name.

Censoring himself, Ben then omits a stanza that describes Genevieve's bosom heaving and her fleeing to him and weeping. The next verse depicts a passionate embrace, so close 'That I might rather feel than see / The swelling of her heart.' Lust is clearly an important part of Ben and Sarah Ann's relationship.

The love affair's not without its difficulties. On the page opposite to Coleridge's Genevieve and her breasts, Ben has copied out a verse by Ceiriog:

O Gwyn ei fyd yr hwn nas gwyr
Am ferch fu'n flinder iddo
Ond wn i ddim yn sicr chwaith
Ai gwyn ei fyd ai peidio.

(Oh, blessèd he who does not trow
A girl who gives him sorrow
Although I do not know for sure
If he be blessed or not.)

There's further suggestion of Trouble in Paradise on another postcard to SA Jones from 155474 Lieutenant Corporal B James, dated 13 March 1918. Two words written large diagonally across the message area: 'Dearest Love'. Someone has rubbed the words in pencil out, with feeling, but left them just visible, like a scar.

I'm surprised that Ben's postcard of 28 December 1918, a month after the end of the war, to Sarah Ann was passed by the censor. Ben notes at the top: 'I am quite well' but the content of the message suggests otherwise. The writing in pencil is very faint and difficult to make out. Is Dacu describing a literal or emotional danger, or both?

> Sorry to say the 'castle' I am afraid is being undermined. I feel it already shaken, and I am very much afraid I will not be able to escape before the collapse of the whole edifice. Still there is one emergency exit, which also may be rendered useless by the debris. It may mean several months of hard labour to make a loophole. Expect nothing.

The couple is, no doubt, eager to be reunited. The postcard continues:

> It is the army. The cup of happiness is always dashed from our lips.

My grandfather's clearly desolate at the end of the war, frustrated and homesick. His return to Sarah Ann must have been rapturous and she fell pregnant quickly, though they married promptly enough to preserve an appearance of respectability, if you didn't look too closely at the dates. Nancy Margretta James was born in December 1919. Tragically she died of pneumonia aged barely six months.

A year later, Megan James, my aunt, was born and, ten years down the line, Eryl. One of the few photos that I have of them as a family is taken in their garden in Llanddewi Brefi. It's dated September 1939, the first month of the Second World War. I'm amazed by how happy the whole family appears to be and struck by how alike Sarah Ann's hands are – pre-rheumatoid arthritis – to Eryl's and, therefore, mine. I'm not used to seeing Mamgu fully dressed and out in the world without a stick. By the time I knew my grandparents, Sarah Ann was bedridden and mean-tempered, Megan was living in America and Eryl was stuck with the consequences. Leighton tells me how much I resemble the young Eryl.

I've only ever heard two good things said about Sarah Ann, my grandmother. Megan Hayes, my mother's cousin, who never utters a bad word about anybody, told me about making toffee with Sarah Ann in the Llanddewi Brefi schoolhouse kitchen. As Mamgu was pulling the mixture, she took a bite out of it, in order to test its consistency. When she drew away, she left her false teeth behind in the confection, causing much merriment.

When Ben James became headmaster of Llanddewi Brefi village school, Sarah Ann was a stay-at-home mother in the schoolhouse next door. She was kind to children from remote farms, who had to walk a long way to school. When they arrived soaked to the skin,

L to R: Sarah Ann, Megan (behind), Eryl and Ben James, September 1939

Mamgu would give them her daughters' clothes to wear while she dried their own on the stove, in time for them to go home.

By the time my grandfather retired, moving to a small bungalow on the edge of the village, Sarah Ann had become permanently bed-ridden and the Mamgu that I knew was a very different person. I recall eating Rice Krispies and sliced banana at their kitchen table, lowering my ear to the bowl in order to listen to the 'snap, crackle and pop!' the grains made in milk, as if it were fairy conversation. The adult presences of Eryl and Dacu hover above me, though I'm concentrating more on rubbing the carvings on the table legs with the tips of my fingers. One morning I recall sitting out in the back garden shelling peas when Rhys, the shepherd on the farm next door, came to visit. This is still my idea of heaven.

The house was divided into two realms. I spent most of my time in the living room where there were Staffordshire dogs in the hearth and a pair of brass crocodile nutcrackers on the mantel shelf. I considered Dacu's sole job to be delighting me. I was still young enough to play the Welsh game for infants, *Gee Ceffyl Bach* ('Gee Little Horse'). Dacu would sit and stretch his legs out in front of him. I would then mount his shins, as if they were a pony and face him. Dacu then obligingly flexed his knees, giving me the sensation of trotting, while we both sang:

Ben James, Gwyneth and Sarah Ann James, 22 August 1960

Gee ceffyl bach yn cario ni'n dau
Dros y mynydd i hela cnau;
Dŵr yn yr afon a'r cerrig yn slic,
Cwympon ni'n dau, wel dyna chi dric!

(Gee little horse who carries us two
Over the mountain to hunt for nuts;
The river is wet, with slippery stones,
We both fell down, well, what a trick!)

With the last line, Dacu would make me fall off the 'horse' in a controlled spill, causing delight, excitement and hilarity. For me, it was the riding while anticipating the fall that gave the most acute pleasure. The reason that the rhyme refers to two people riding, rather than one, is that even though Dacu was, technically, more horse than rider in the game, the way that he and I both looked each other in the eye, concentrating hard on both riding and singing, made him a centaur. This close attention, coupled with the actions, made me scream for him to do it again and again, for as long as his patience and elderly knees could bear it. I would have loved to gallop along a white cloud and jump over the moon with my Dacu.

Our bond was the closer because I was placed to sleep in his bed, which I thought was an excellent arrangement. I never remembered Dacu coming in at night but, at dawn, I'd examine his sleeping face in minute detail, highly amused by his snoring. His profile was a beloved mountain range to me, each peak of which I knew by its exact, dear name in Welsh: '*talcen, trwyn, gwefus, gên*' ('forehead, nose, lip, chin'). I regarded the alarm clock on the dressing table as a living being, its loud tick part of a conversation in which I was taking part but without fully understanding it. When I tired of the clock, I'd wake Dacu by singing, in turn, every single song I'd learned from nursery school. *Insi Winsi Copyn* ('Incy Wincy Spider') climbed up the wall many times, to be swept away by the rain. I'd ask the snowdop ('*Lili Wen Fach*') where on earth she had come from in the middle of winter. Dacu dozed and grunted. I swung the light switch of the pink reading lamp clamped to the headboard, hoping to wake him up with the clatter. He resisted for as long as he could.

The second realm in the house was Sarah Ann's sick room. She suffered from generalised malaise for years before taking to her bed for good. Eryl bore the brunt of her mother's deteriorating health as she grew up and always blamed this upbringing for her own black moods. It was as if she were being possessed by Sarah Ann and there was nothing she could do about it.

Mamgu's room was dark, like something out of a Ceredigion Gothic tale. I always entered the room with trepidation. Sarah Ann wasn't the kind of patient to welcome visits from young children or let them snuggle in on her bed, like kittens, to keep her company. She had thick hair that had been crinkly, but which was now cut in a straight, severe bob with a clip to hold the fringe back. She wore a gored crocheted cape, made of jewel-like reds, blues and greens. It fell in the same scallop pattern as the curtain that covered the screen in our local cinema. Other times she wore a bed jacket in lemon yellow, another in blue; these came with matching bed-socks. Ribbons threaded through the top around swollen ankles and feet with reptilian dried skin, which horrified me. Mamgu's hands were deformed by arthritis, bony and bent at an impossible angle, like coastal trees bullied horizontal by the wind. She had been advised to continue to knit, to keep her fingers flexible, but, characteristically, had refused. All in all, in her short cape, Mamgu looked like Pope Innocent X painted by Velázquez; emotionally, she felt like Francis Bacon's screaming pontiff.

Around the bed lay the paraphernalia of the unwell. There was the thick walking stick made of dark wood. Over the bed slid an invalid's tray and, on the bedside table, a Lucozade bottle wrapped in the yellow cellophane, gathered at the top, that made it an object of fascination. I used to take the cellophane off and peer through the amber filter, like the night-driving glasses that my father wore. Before it was rebranded as a sports drink, Lucozade was exclusively used by invalids and was to be seen in hospitals alongside bunches of flowers and fruit. It was, basically, pop for the ill but was treated as soft medicine. I sensed that it had something to do with the vexed question of bowels.

I learned years later that Sarah Ann was suffering from *lupus erythematosus*, an autoimmune disease that leads to chronic inflammation of joints, skin, kidneys, heart, lungs, blood vessels and brain (though not all of these in every patient). The disease was named the Wolf by Paracelsus, who used it to refer to any injury to the skin of the lower limbs because it reminded him of the bite of a wolf. So, Sarah Ann was both Red Riding Hood's Grandma and the predator that had eaten her and, disguised as an invalid, taken her place.

To the right of the bed stood a frightening piece of furniture: the commode. Made of wood, its seat lifted to reveal a china pot which I knew was to be dreaded. There was a sickly orangey smell that I've never forgotten and didn't encounter again until my parents reached the end of their lives.

How do you live in a poisoned home atmosphere? As Sarah Ann became progressively more unwell, Ben James retreated into his work. He was a gifted teacher. On graduating from Trinity College, Carmarthen, he did his probationary year in Gilfach Goch. The report on him noted:

> His discipline is firm but at the same time kind and just. He succeeds in enlisting the confidence of the children in his charge, thus getting the maximum amount of work out of them.

The same can be said of Eryl as a teacher. Ben James was tireless in his contribution to the community. An article in the local paper marking his retirement noted that:

> For many years he was secretary of the Tregaron Teachers' Provident Society, for which services he was presented with an illuminated address and other gifts; secretary of the Village Hall Committee, clerk of the Parish Council and Burial Board, and secretary of the Thomas and Ratcliffe Charity Fund.
>
> He was a faithful member of Bethesda C.M. [Calvinistic Methodist] Chapel, where he was a Sunday School teacher, a deacon and treasurer.

In addition, Ben also helped people to fill in official forms, as needed. He also became an obsessive recorder of weather, perhaps as an antidote to the volatile atmospheric conditions at home. In a notebook with a red marbled cover, he made daily entries on the weather in Llanddewi Brefi from 1939 to 1950. It resembles the migraine log I now keep, in order to track various treatments and brain fog.

As a poet, I used this record to riff on what might have been happening in my grandparents' marriage and voiced it in my mother's persona:

'My father was distant ...'

Faced with perpetual winter in the house
he turned his attention, the greater part of love,
outside and kept a daily Weather book,
an act of faith that things were on the move,
despair can change. His neat Remarks
show him a connoisseur of Wet
in months so boring I suspect a code
in 'Fair but rather sultry in the E',
and 'Wintry showers', outlined in red.
The highlight is: 'A cloudburst in Cwmdu,
extensive damage caused.' It's plain –
a light, then gentler, later stiffening breeze,
a week in July of 'very BRIGHT'.
No comments then for several days.
He was an adulterer with light.

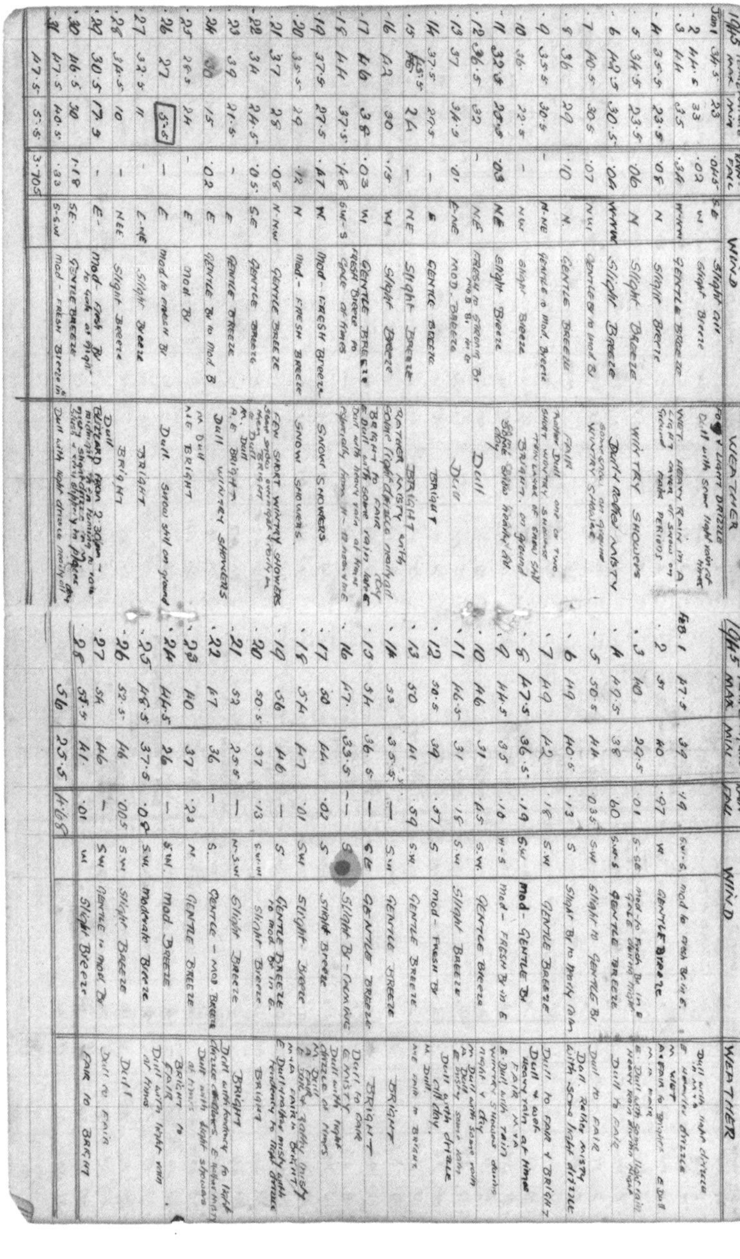

1945	Temperature Max	Temperature Min	Rainfall	Wind		Weather
Jan 1	34.5	23	.045	S.E	Slight air	Fog & light drizzle
2	44.5	33	.02	W	Slight Breeze	Dull with some light rain at times
3	44	35	.34	W-NW	Gentle Breeze	Wet. Heavy rain in A. Light layer of snow on ground. Rain periods
4	35.5	23.5	.08	N	Slight Breeze	
5	34.5	23.5	.06	N	Slight Breeze	Wintry showers
6	42.5	30.5	.04	W-NW	Slight Breeze	Dull & rather misty
7	40.5	30.5	.07	NW	Gentle Br to mod. Br	Some snow on ground. Wintry showers
8	36	29	.10	N.	Gentle Breeze	Fair
9	35.5	30.5	–	N-NE	Gentle to mod. Breeze	Rather dull. One or two short wintry showers
10	36	22.5	–	NW	Slight Breeze	Thin layer of snow still on ground. Bright.
11	32.5	28.5	.03	NE	Slight Breeze	Some snow nearly all day
12	36.5	32	–	NE	Fresh to strong Br mod Br in E	Dull
13	37	34.5	.01	E-NE	Mod. Breeze	Dull
14	37.5	27.5	–	E	Gentle Breeze	Bright
15	45.5	24	–	NE	Slight Breeze	Bright
16	42	30	.15	W	Slight Breeze	Rather misty with some light drizzle nearly all day
17	46	38	.03	W	Gentle Breeze	Bright to fair. E Dull with some rain later
18	44	37.5	.48	SW-S	Fresh Breeze to Gale at times	Dull with heavy rain at times especially from 4 – 12 noontime
19	37.5	27.5	.47	W	Mod - Fresh Breeze	Snow showers
20	35.5	29	.12	N	Mod. - Fresh Breeze	Snow showers
21	37	28	.08	N-NW	Gentle Breeze	Few short wintry showers
22	34	24.5	.05	S.E	Gentle Breeze	Some snow overnight & early m. then bright & dull
23	39	21.5	–	E	Gentle Breeze	M. Dull A.E Bright
24	30	15	.02	E	Gentle Br to mod. B	Dull wintry showers
25	28.5	24	–	E	Mod. Br	M Dull A/E Bright
26	27	5.5	–	E	Mod. to fresh Br	Dull. Snow still on ground
27	32.5	11	–	E-NE	Slight Breeze	Bright
28	34.5	10	–	NEE	Slight Breeze	Bright
29	30.5	17.5	–	E-	Mod - fresh Br to gale at night	Dull. Blizzard from 2.30pm – midnight then turning to rain
30	46.5	30	1.18	SE	Gentle Breeze	Misty slight drizzle in m. Slush & very slippery in places
31	47.5	40.5	.33	S-S.W	Mod - Fresh Breeze in E	Dull with light drizzle nearly all day
	47.5	5.5	3.705			

1945	Temperature Max	Temperature Min	Rainfall	Wind		Weather
Feb. 1	47.5	39	.19	S.W-S.	Mod to fresh Br in E.	Dull with light drizzle in M & A. E heavier drizzle
2	51	40	.97	W	Gentle Breeze	M wet. A Fair to bright. E Dull
3	40	29.5	.01	S-SE	Mod to fresh Br in E. Gale during night	M-A Fair. E Dull with some light rain. Heavy rain during night
4	49.5	38	.60	S.W-S	Gentle Breeze	Dull to fair
5	50.5	44	.035	S.W	Slight to Gentle Br	Dull to fair
6	49	40.5	.13	S	Slight Br to mostly calm	Dull. Rather misty with some light drizzle
7	49	42	.18	S.W	Gentle Breeze	Dull to fair & bright
8	47.5	36.5	.19	S.W	Mod - Gentle Br	Dull & wet. Heavy rain at times
9	44.5	35	.10	W-S	Mod - Fresh Br in E	Fair M & A. E Dull with rain
10	46	31	.45	S.W.	Gentle Breeze	Wintry showers during night & day
11	46.5	31	.18	S.W	Slight Breeze	M Dull with some rain. A Dull. E Misty some rain
12	50.5	39	.57	S	Mod - Fresh Br	Dull with drizzle all day
13	50	41	.59	S.W	Gentle Breeze	M. Dull. A/E Fair to bright
14	53	35.5	—	S.W	Gentle Breeze	Bright
15	54	36.5	—	SE	Gentle Breeze	Bright
16	47	33.5	—	S	Slight Br - calming	Dull to fair. E Misty
17	50	44	.02	S	Slight Breeze	Dull with light drizzle at times
18	54	47	.01	SW	Slight Breeze	M Dull. A Fair. E Dull & rather misty
19	56	46	—	S	Gentle Breeze to mod. Br in E.	M & A Fair & Bright. E Dull & rather misty with tendency to light drizzle
20	50.5	37	.13	S.W-W	Slight Breeze	Bright
21	52	25.5	—	N-S.W	Slight Breeze	Bright
22	47	36	—	S.	Gentle - Mod Breeze	Dull with tendency to light drizzle at times. E rather misty
23	40	37	.23	N	Gentle Breeze	Dull with light showers at times
24	44.5	26	—	S.W.	Mod Breeze	Bright to fair
25	48.5	37.5	.08	S.W	Moderate Breeze	Dull with light rain at times
26	52.5	46	.005	S.W	Slight Breeze	Dull
27	54	46	—	S.W	Gentle to mod. Br	Dull to fair
28	53.5	41	.01	W	Slight Breeze	Fair to bright
	56	25.5	4.68			

Ben James's weather log

Once, Sarah Ann sent Ben out to find apricots in midwinter. This impossible task belongs not to the reality of post-war west Wales but to the realm of fairy tales. It speaks to me of the desperate desire of the chronically ill for comfort and the equally futile attempts of their carers to provide it.

One day, in Cardiff, two policemen came to the door with the news that Ben James had died suddenly of a stroke, aged only seventy. This must have been before we had a phone in the house. I was five and, after the officers had gone, I remember hugging Eryl as she sobbed with shock. She was wearing the short-sleeved jumper of a beige twinset which she'd knitted herself. I can feel its texture now as I reached up to comfort her.

A few weeks later, after the funeral, I ran ahead of my parents into my grandparents' house and, while they were unloading bags after the long journey west, burst into Sarah Ann's room. The question of care for invalid Mamgu had become pressing and was much discussed by my parents. I wanted to be the first to tell her the exciting news that she was coming to live with us in Cardiff and that I was pleased to welcome her.

I wasn't prepared for the wail that rose from the figure in the bed. I saw the shout unfurling from Sarah Ann's mouth like a leather whip and unspooling up towards the ceiling. She screamed:

'*Eryl! Beth yw hyn am …?*'

('Eryl! What's this about …?')

I was terrified by the noise of the argument and by the shocking mismatch between my good intentions and their disastrous consequences. My mother rushed in, saw me next to the bed, worked out what had happened. Then she began to scream at me, asking:

'*Pam yn y byd ddwedest di …?*'

('Why on earth did you tell her …?')

I had no idea that what I'd heard was meant to be secret. I ran and hid, terrified and inconsolable.

It's not only physical looks that are passed between generations. If you listen carefully, you can perceive the echoes of how previous adults have spoken to each other. In fact, it's just as impossible to avoid those tones of voice and sentiments as to change an inherited build or gait. Parents, despite their strongest resolutions, end up sounding like their own when they talk to their children. What I can hear in my recollection of the exchange above isn't so much the words as the start of phrases, their 'tune', the pitch and *sol-ffa* of blame and rage.

Recent research has shown that exposure to verbal abuse is far more serious than previously thought. A study by the *British Medical Journal Open* found, for example, that, of 20,556 UK residents, those who'd been verbally abused were twice as likely as those who had not to use cannabis and to end up in jail.[4] The vitriol wasn't so much in the words, but in the tone, which was poisonous and frightening. Verbal abuse is a hall of mirrors, victims turning into perpetrators, whether they want to or not. Sarah Ann must have learned that kind of speech from Crugeryr, so I look at the photograph of my great-grandfather, Thomas Jones, and great-grandmother, Anne Nansi Jones, and wonder what Sarah Ann and the Crugeryr clock witnessed in the mid-nineteenth century.

While Mamgu was still alive, I could hear the original theme behind the verbal catches that became Eryl's way of talking to me when she was angry with me and her guard was down. If daily events were the recitatives, these were the arias my mother sang to me:

'*Er mwyn Dyn, pam odd rhaid i ti?*'
('For God's sake, why did you have to?')
'*Gwilym, dwedwch wrth y ferch!*'
('Gwilym, tell the girl!')
'*Ti'n hollol* impractical.'
('You're totally impractical.')

---

4 'Shouting at children can be as damaging as physical or sexual abuse, study says', *The Guardian*, 2 October 2023.

'*O, beth yw'r iws?*'
('Oh, what's the use?')
'*Cer o 'ngolwg i.*'
('Get out of my sight.')

And it's catching. There's a tone of voice that I use, when riled, that Leighton tells me 'cuts like a knife'. It comes out of my mouth when I'm especially irritated or frustrated. It's vicious, mean, and has no regard for other people, whom it treats like fools. It comes from a deep fear of getting things wrong and being harshly criticised for it. This voice does not have my consent to be in my mind but it's the score of a dreaded music, hard-wired into the unguarded part of my brain. I try my best not to use it but, when that sound comes out of my mouth, it feels totally natural, way deeper than my mother tongue.

Leighton is, rightly, robust in his defence against this tone of voice and its presence isn't tolerated in our relationship. But it takes a toll because it happens so unexpectedly.

—*What about getting an exorcist?*

—*You, again?*

—*You go to any lengths not to behave like Eryl, don't you? Why didn't she do the same?*

—*You're so judgemental.*

—*You're not judgemental enough for your own good.*

—*Eryl's a victim too.*

—*She knew how awful it was to be spoken to in such a way and she did it to you anyway.*

—*But she couldn't help it.*

—*Always, there's always a choice.*

I can drive that monster back into its lair. Exorcising it is impossible, but I do my best to starve it of oxygen, air time in my mouth. I'm determined that this speech infection, this ear-worm of rage and disappointment stops here. I will not be trapped in such a catch song. It's a toxic inheritance, but I have it, whether I want it or not. What you say and how you say it ruins lives.

I heard a lot of that wailing and mother-daughter antagonism after Mamgu, accompanied by the dreaded commode, came to live with us in Cardiff in 1967, the last years of her life. My parents turned our living room into a sick room, reproducing the gloomy set from the bungalow in Llanddewi Brefi. Sarah Ann did not make life easy for herself or for her daughter. Lifting her overweight mother resulted in Eryl suffering a slipped disc in her back. Sarah Ann would throw her pills in the commode, making Eryl think that they were passing, undigested, right through her system. There was frequent screaming. We girls were told to keep away and we did.

One day, when I'm eight, I forget that Mamgu is living with us and, by mistake, burst into the living room. Mam is giving her a bed-bath. Mamgu was sitting, facing the door, the top half of her body naked. Her skin is yellow (from the kidney failure that will appear on her death certificate as the cause of death), so Mamgu's body looked as if it were made out of melting butter. Her breasts are empty triangles of skin, hanging down to her waist. Both women scream:

'*Cer o 'ma!*'

('Get out of here!')

I beat a swift retreat, shocked by what I've seen.

This image rose up from dark waters to haunt me years later. When I was a second-year student at university, I suffered a nervous breakdown. One memorable night, I can't breathe, or move. This is the end of eighteen months of intense conflict with my parents. I feel reduced to a ghost, with no will of my own. Then my distress takes a sinister turn. I notice that there's a red spot, like an insect bite, on my leg in exactly the same place as my mother has a mark. This makes me hysterical because, to my mind, it shows that I'm turning into her and, behind her, Sarah Ann. I feel that I've inherited that wolf's bite that will condemn me to destroying myself and others with my bitterness. I no longer know which wounds are mine and which belong to others.

Then reality becomes hallucinatory. I half remember a fairy tale in which a crone puts a young woman in a bath in a marble cistern, in which lily pads grow. Then, as part of an enchantment, the hag places toads on the naked girl's breast, and along her body. I imagine Mamgu doing this to me, marking me with her poison. I've searched for the fairy tale but can't find it now; it seems such an odd thing to make up. The fantasy was half frightening and half erotic, being trapped in the magic world of a wicked grandmother, a vision of passivity which was strangely seductive. Soon, I felt that I would be speaking in toads and frogs.

I can't remember if the princess escapes from the witch or not. It strikes me now that I always dreaded *becoming* my tormentor more than being her victim because I'd already survived that for so long. This gave me, I think, a better chance of ultimate escape, but meant I was reckless about how much damage I could bear before I stood up, stepped out of the pool, naked and dripping, to inspect my wounds.

Not all the Crugeryr girls were as dark in temperament as Sarah Ann was to become. I used to enjoy visiting one of the younger sisters, Marged Jane, in her house in Talgarreg, as she was full of fun. My great-aunt looked like her older sister, Sarah Ann, but in a major key. She lived in 'Eryri', a small house on the main road through Talgarreg. I remember her sitting in her kitchen, laughing. Flypaper twisted like DNA's double helix down from the ceiling. Marged Jane was a big woman, dressed in the rural uniform of an overall covering her clothes and a cardigan over that. When she sat, I could see where her stockings ended just past her knees and, despite a petticoat, an expanse of bulging inner thigh the colour of uncooked pastry. She had two delightful black miniature poodles who jumped up to kiss us girls. I loved her rich Cardiganshire Welsh.

My parents bought the Crugeryr grandfather clock from Marged Jane. This robust timepiece had been transported from the farm on the back of a tractor to my great-aunt's tiny cottage. Gwilym hired a van to transport the clock from Talgarreg to Cardiff. Before leaving Marged Jane's house, he wrote a typically meticulous list of instructions to himself:

> TO DISMANTLE GRANDFATHER
> 1) Take off face case – pull forward
> 2) Lift up weight to about 6" from top & remove weight
> 3) Remove pendulum – lock in from side & take out pin – IF transporting – tie pendulum to length of wood for support
> 4) Pull clock face & works forwards – lift up forwards
>
> To assemble –
> Reverse the above procedure

As he was reassembling the clock in our hall, Gwilym noticed that the pendulum was crooked, so he straightened it. From then on, the mechanism never worked for more than seven minutes at a go. It stood silent in my parents' house for over forty years, stalled.

A Welsh-language writer who was reputed to have second sight once told me that every poet has another from the past standing at her shoulder, helping her. It's 2013 and Leighton is in hospital for a hip replacement. When I go to visit the evening after the operation, he's lying with his gown half off, suffering from morphine itch, and high as a kite. He tells me to go over to the other side of the ward to speak to an ex-footballer who's having his knee replaced. He's a spiritualist. So, presented with someone else who offers himself as psychic, I ask him who my poetic spirit guide is. His answer stunned me:

'Your grandmother.'

I'm sceptical but the man continues briskly. He tells me that there's a photograph of Mamgu, my mother and me together (I don't have one but, by writing this chapter, I'm creating one). Sarah Ann died of a heart attack (no, it was kidney failure) but had lots of other health problems (yes, lupus is a disease that attacks multiple organs). As a guardian she's full of energy, but is no longer with Dacu (probably a good thing for both of them). She's telling me to decide if I'm really going to give being a writer a go (I'm never confident). The word Constance suggests itself to him (George Herbert has a poem called 'Constancie', but this is only my association). He asks if I had a problem (his tone suggested sexual) with my father (no). There's a brother miscarried (Eryl did suffer a lost pregnancy). My guardian isn't the type to be pushed into a corner (damn right) but I might be (yup). I'm going to make it as a poet, but should write prayers for all the nations (I can't think of a less fashionable idea in the poetry marketplace right now, so, perversely, the idea appeals to me.). My grandmother sits at the end of my bed at night and, to show me she's there, will turn a photograph upstairs around the wrong way (she hasn't so far, but I'll keep looking).

I don't think that Sarah Ann is reaching out to me from the afterlife, but this encounter jolts me into reframing my inheritance from her. Until then, I've considered Sarah Ann's behaviour in the family as a curse. But as a muse? Who says that inspiration has to be agreeable, or even likeable? Ferocity, if it's directed not at you but at your adversaries, is a powerful defence. Sarah Ann, who I've considered as an enemy for so long, is the last person I'd look to for artistic help. Since being so chronically ill myself, I also know the fevered originality of an invalid's ideas and what frustrated vitality she possesses. Being out of the world requires thinking that's not stale or mainstream. It has to be powerful, original and utterly sincere, in order to stop you from drowning in your own malaise. To listen to a clock whose movement ticks and chimes is to hang a bell around time's neck. It doesn't stop the day hunting you but it does make you aware of it getting ready to pounce, with enough warning so that you can move out of your own way.

Now I can think of my muse as a pair of false teeth, detached from their historical owner but, nevertheless, biting down on sugar. And, as on the Tate and Lyle syrup tin, out of strength, if you can stand it, comes forth sweetness.

I had claimed the Crugeryr clock imaginatively in a poem years before I inherited it. In Welsh, a clock is said to walk, a formulation which combines the two dimensions of time and space, turning the instrument into a marker of space-time. I imagined claiming the clock from Talgarreg in a poem included in my collection *Tair Mewn Un* ('Three in One') :

Yr Etifedd

Wedi marw fy modryb,
deuthum mewn car
i gyrchu'r hen gloc yn ofalus o'r tŷ.
Roedd y car bach yn llawn
a 'doedd dim amdani
ond tynnu'r pendil cam a'm rhoi i
i orwedd fel corff yn y casyn cain
a thrin fy etifeddiaeth fel arch
yr holl ffordd adref.

Ar hyd y lôn
plygodd y perthi i ddangos eu parch
at yr ymadawedig. A'r tu fewn
i'r golofn, yn brydlon, fy bydrwn i,
pob eiliad yn dic yn fy mherfedd coeth,
yn cadw amser yn berffaith. Cysgais yn drwm.

Taith ddigon doniol. Ond wedi cyrraedd yn ôl
roedd fy atgyfodiad yn ddigon o farn
a minnau'n teimlo symudiad y plwm
yn fy ymysgaroedd. Dim ond hyn a hyn
mae pob cloc yn cerdded. Rwy'n cyfrif pob cam.

(The Heir

When my aunt died,
I came in a car
to fetch the old clock from the house, with care.
The small car was full,
so there was no choice
but to pull out the crooked pendulum
and place me, like a corpse in the beautiful case,
to treat my inheritance like a coffin
all the way home.

Along the lanes
the hedgerows bowed in respect
to the departed. And inside
the column, punctual, I rotted,
each second a tick inside my gut,
keeping time perfectly. I fell fast asleep.
A curious journey. But arriving home,
my resurrection was a sight to see,
and I felt the movement of the weight
in my intestines. Every clock can only walk
so far. Each step, I count.)

It's striking to me now that I'd imagined the clock case as a coffin, as if family time had a hand in dictating how I'm to die. Genetics play a part, of course, but the imagination is the one force that can disrupt chronology.

When we move into my parents' house, Leighton finds a clock repairer, who brings the Crugeryr clock back to life. I can hear its weighty tick now, hugely comforting, like the beating of Leighton's heart next to me in bed. This is the metronome by which we live our life, the soundtrack of our home together. The clock's walk has been a witness to my extended family's use of language for centuries. Its sound incorporates us into the many generations who've lived and worked to the same steady tread, and puts us in a broader company than my nuclear family, with the anonymous predecessors who also heard it chime through the night. It's an inherited rhythm, well on the way to being poetry. I'm living to a sound that's centuries old, which gives me a more open space than my immediate family in which to breathe.

First thing every morning, I watch Leighton coming down the stairs and, before thinking of coffee, he addresses the Crugeryr clock, pulling up the eighteen-inch-long weight that's fallen in a controlled manner on its chain and landed on the floor. It sounds like a person raising a sack of flour in a warehouse, like hanging the corpse of yesterday, so that we have another twenty-four hours together.

Chapter 2
MISTAKEN IDENTITIES

When my younger sister Marian is born two years after me, our Great Auntie Muriel visits us in Cardiff to admire the new baby. She had nursed in France during the First World War and then became a companion to Mrs Stoddart, a concert pianist who retired to Sunningdale, Berkshire, and had a pipe organ in her sitting room. Muriel, bearing a certain resemblance to Henry VII, has a sharp and observant eye. As my father is about to take a photo of us in the garden, my sister in a shawl, he urges us to stand closer together, and I cuddle in alongside my mother. Muriel exclaims:

'Look at that! The baby's pushing Gwyneth away!'

It's more usual for the older child, jealous of the attention being given to the new arrival, to be the one rejecting the other.

—*That's not what's happening here at all!*

—*What do you know? You weren't even there.*

—*Was too. Baby has picked up on what Eryl feels and is enacting it for her.*

—*It's Eryl pushing me away?*

—*Think of how closely attuned a breastfeeding mother and baby are.*

When Eryl repeats the story, which she thinks is funny, over the years, she plays the baby part, never the mother. She turns her face away from the implied me, like a ballerina's mimed gesture rejecting a lover, with a moue of disgust. Get away from me.

—It happened that early. You never had a chance.
—But WHY? What did I do that was so wrong?
—Nothing. She was rejecting somebody else.

My aunt, Megan James, was born in 1920, the year after Ben and Sarah Ann James lost their first daughter. Eryl appeared a decade later, in 1930, '*cyw bach gwaelod y nyth*' ('small chick at the bottom of the nest'), an unexpected late pregnancy. Such children are often indulged more than their elder siblings but Sarah Ann told Eryl that she was a mistake. On one visit to Talgarreg, Marged Jane described Megan, '*fel deryn bach y tô*' ('like a little house sparrow') when she came to visit Crugeryr as a child and commented that I resembled her. Mam held a silence, which I heard. Marged Jane couldn't have said anything worse, and I knew, obscurely, that I would pay for the compliment.

One photograph of the sisters speaks eloquently to me. Megan and Eryl are both wearing best party dresses for a semi-formal family photo of the girls. I calculate that Eryl is nine or ten years old, so the date is about 1940. Both sisters' dresses are home-made but the red velvet Eryl is wearing is a hand-me-down. Its main feature is a row of pearl buttons. Rather than running down the middle of her torso, as it should, the line of buttons is offset. The dress has been altered to fit a growing girl, so perhaps there wasn't enough material in the bodice seams both for her size and to reproduce the garment's original style. This is the kind of wardrobe humiliation that mortifies a child and the way I read the photo is that Eryl's furious. I have a faint memory of Eryl telling me that she was but, of course, I may be imposing my interpretation of family history on the snapshot of a moment. What I see is that Eryl's pique is

Velvet dresses

not only about the buttons, but about 'Megan always being the favourite', which became a lifelong resentment. Megan, with her grown-up mother-of-pearl buttons plumb down the front of her dress, is serenely unaware of the turmoil next to her.

In this photograph Megan is probably about to leave home to study medicine at Cardiff University. In 1942, she won a Rockefeller Scholarship to continue her studies in the US. This may be a 'best' photograph her parents took of her with Eryl before she left

Cardiganshire to make the Atlantic crossing, a hazardous voyage, due to German U-boat patrols. Megan crossed safely and completed her studies at a Chicago medical school. She never came back to live in Wales. If I'm right about this being a farewell photograph, Eryl's bad feelings towards Megan would have been complicated by fear of being left alone with their parents, whose marriage was far from easy. Rather than avoiding the favouritism shown by her parents towards Megan, Eryl reproduced it. Eryl's jealousy of her sister was to become a poisonous inheritance for me.

In America, Megan met and married Bill Tanner, who took her back to his hometown of Danville, Illinois, where she practised as a paediatrician and a family doctor. Between them, they delivered or treated most of the town's population. In addition, they had five sons of their own. Annual Christmas photographs would arrive, showing Bill and Megan surrounded by their growing brood of athletic, high-achieving sons, among them a cosmetic dental surgeon and an astronaut. All were swimmers, with twins David and Joe training with Olympic champion Mark Spitz. David became a professional swim coach and exercise physiologist while Joe worked for NASA and helped repair the Hubble Space Telescope.

It seems to me that, in photographs of us Lewises on holiday as a family, my sister is most often next to Eryl and often touching, whereas I'm off a little to the side. I'm older, of course, and more curious about the world. It's not obligatory for a parent to like their children equally – there are natural temperamental alliances and preferences.

—There you go, making excuses again. Don't let her off the hook.

—Affection isn't something that you can control.

—Eryl knew what it was like to be rejected but she did it anyway to you. It's basic justice to make all your children feel safe and approved of.

—It wasn't deliberate.

—And what has that done to you?

—I wish that I could claw off my face, get rid of myself.

In the book of Genesis, Jacob deceives Isaac, his dying father, out of the blessing meant for his older twin Esau (the 'hairy man'). Impersonating his brother, he would have heard the tenderness in his father's voice and known that it was not intended for him:

> Ah, the smell of my son
> is like the smell of a field
> that the Lord has blessed.

One day, after she was widowed and nearly blind, I glimpse another emotional country within the family. Eryl is expecting a visit from Marian and has left the front door unlocked. I pop by without phoning first, shout as I enter the house and make my way into the dark sitting room. Eryl greets me in an intimate tone of voice that's totally new to me. This tender and confiding conversation continues until my mother realises her mistake. Immediately, her guard is up again but not before I have a tantalising taste of what it's like to be my sister in her eyes. Just as I knew that I wasn't Megan, I also knew not to take this hostility personally.

As Eryl became more frail, her preference became more overt. I don't think that I've resented my sister for the difference in Eryl's attitude towards us, because it wasn't her doing. I've also observed that being the favourite brings its own problems. Marian and I would take turns in making sure that Eryl had everything she needed. I had been working away and my sister was exhausted. It was my weekend to attend to our mother. I phoned to say that I was coming round.

'I want Marian.'

'Marian can't come, she's resting. You've got me.'

Eryl shouted down the phone:

'I WANT MARIAN!'

One day, towards the end of Eryl's life, the subject of her preference came up between us. We were sitting in her kitchen when she said, complacently:

'I've always treated you and your sister exactly the same.'

Financially, my parents were generous to us all our lives, especially during the long years of our education. When we were young, Eryl was scrupulously even-handed between us – doll for doll, present for present. If she made us clothes, we both had new dresses and sweaters, often matching, at the same rate. Eryl stressed her fairness so often, though, that I felt that it was a conscious effort. Marian had the knack of drawing Eryl's indulgence, whereas I tended only to infuriate her.

By the time of this late conversation, I had removed myself from the arena between me and Eryl, but couldn't let this lie pass. Besides, I was curious.

'That's not quite true, is it?'

Eryl paused. Because I wasn't being confrontational she could afford to admit: 'No.'

This was a rare moment of openness, so I went for broke. Gwilym was already dead, Eryl was ailing, so opportunities to ask important questions were becoming scarce. Here was a chance to have an honest answer. I kept my voice deliberately casual.

'As a matter of interest, why did you find me so difficult to deal with?' I really wanted to know and hoped for an end-of-life-nothing-to-lose degree of self-reflection on her part.

I expected Eryl to cite examples of my bad behaviour. She could have reproached me for my stubbornness or defiance, both of which are prominent in my repertoire of liabilities. Certain children are hard to handle but, on the whole, I thought I'd been a compliant daughter – respectful, conscientious academically, mostly honest, no criminal activities, unplanned pregnancies or notable delinquency. She thought for a moment, then said:

'You were always so bright.'

My mother's alleged difficulty with me was my being 'bright', which not only isn't a behaviour, but a quality generally considered desirable. *Bright*?

And what kind of bright did she mean? The same word denotes both a capacity for hopefulness and a form of intelligence. Neither of these are qualities that can be altered, even if you want to. The ability to see clearly is, furthermore, a paradoxical gift. Rather than being something to be treated as an object of pride, its end result is only ever to draw attention to the world beyond itself. It's a window and the value of glass lies in its degree of transparency. The real virtue associated with brightness isn't possessing it in the first place, but the willingness to keep the pane dirt-free, so that it can do its work and let in light. Simone Weil catches this paradox exactly:

> There is nothing nearer to true humility than the intelligence. It is impossible to be proud of our intelligence at the moment when we are really exercising it. Moreover, when we do exercise it we are not attached to it, for we know that, even if we became an idiot the following instant and remained so for the rest of our life, the truth would continue unchanged.

There was no point talking further to Eryl about the past. The problem, as ever, was me. I was wearing the better velvet dress, leaving Mam with the off-centre buttons. All those years of emotional abuse: I'd made her do it.

My father, Gwilym Lewis, was born in 1926 to David, a coal miner, and Mary Ann Lewis in Ogmore Vale. I found a tiny booklet of Psalms, the paper's grain impregnated with coal dust; it was so well used that my grandfather must have been in the habit of taking the book underground with him, for comfort, as the hot earth pressed down. My grandmother, Mary Ann (who had hair so long she could sit on it, not one strand ever turned white), was the daughter of Charles Williams, minister of the Hermon, a Calvinistic Methodist chapel in Ogmore. He had been part of the 1904 Methodist Revival in south Wales. When he was widowed, Charles Williams – portly, bearded – came to live in the Lewis home at 28 Meadow St., a double bay-fronted property just uphill of the main road. Enid, my aunt, ten years younger than my father, was Charles Williams's favourite. Despite the decade's difference between their ages, Gwilym and Enid were close throughout their lives. No jealousy there, then. One day, Charles Williams and young Enid were walking up the mountain, when he slipped into the stream. She laughed so much that even she fell out of favour with him. Not long after, Charles Williams remarried a well-off widow and published a memoir called *Y Deugain Mlynedd Hyn* ('These Forty Years'), conflating the traditional Old Testament period of trial with his own life in the south Wales valleys.

Aged seventeen and against his mother's will, Gwilym volunteered for the Royal Navy. He trained in Scotland as an early radar engineer, when that was the cutting-edge technology which gave Britain a crucial edge in Second World War aerial combat. He told a terrifying story of a fellow mechanic who was trapped in a radar unit as big as a room: when the device was activated, the person was killed stone dead. Seeing in the dark comes at a price, if you don't keep a respectful distance from the energies.

After training on board HMS *Diomede*, Gwilym went out to Australia via the Panama Canal to join HMS *Assistance*. She was a converted Liberty ship, used as a mobile repair unit so that vessels didn't have to come into port for maintenance. In a letter from Sydney, dated 18 July 1945, Gwilym thanks his mother for sending him a clothes brush (though he'd since bought another) and a cake which, alas, wasn't very tasty. In order to supplement severe wartime rationing at home:

> *gyrrais ddau parsel tua wythnos yn ol. Oedd un yn llawn bwyd – dipyn o siwgwr a ffrwyth sŷch, – ac yn yr un arall mae pedwar par o hosannau* silk, *â dau bŵys o* sultanas *ac yr un faint o gyrrants. 'Mae dau bâr o'r 'sannau yn anrheg Nadolig i Auntie Muriel, a'r ddau arall i Mam.*
>
> (I sent two parcels about a week ago. One was full of food – quite a lot of sugar and dried fruit, – and in the other one are four pairs of silk stockings, two pounds of sultanas and the same amount of currants. Two of the pairs of stockings are a Christmas present to Auntie Muriel, and the other two for Mam.)
>
> (18 July 1945)

The war ends in September 1945, to celebrations in Sydney and in Ogmore. By October, Gwilym is bored and struggling to find something amusing to say. Eryl always used to warn us not to believe a word Gwilym said in any letter he wrote, because he was always more intent on creating an amusing story than recounting about actual circumstances. On this occasion in Australia, Gwilym's friend, Geoff, takes over:

> Well, Gwilym has run out of words, for once in his young lifetime, so I thought that I would take over for him. It was more of an ordeal watching him thinking of something to say, and anyway, I must try and save wear and tear of his grey matter! To write something of interest I can only say he is in the best of health, living like a lord, and, in spite of his protests, growing as fat as a little porker!
>
> (23 October 1945)

Somehow, Gwilym acquired a Japanese submarine radio case, in which he subsequently kept his leather sewing kit for the repair of belts, furniture and shoes. I still have the box and its contents. He also served on board HMS *Loch Glendhu*, whose 'purpose of voyage' was to escort the former Japanese ship *Shofoku Maru* to Cheribon (present-day Cirebon, Java), 140 miles east of Batavia (Jakarta). On board were 460 Indonesians who, according to one of his letters, 'are not considered entirely trustworthy'.

By January 1946, HMS *Assistance* has reached Singapore, where a good peacetime boredom was punctuated by the hazards of being a radio mechanic:

> The most interesting item of news is as follows:– Geoff while working on a set the other day was unfortunate enough to touch a contact bearing 4,000 volts & executed two back somersaults before losing consciousness. He came around in a few minutes however & after a day's rest in sick bay is now as full

> of beans as ever, but much more cautious. It is the fact that one is continually wet with perspiration that makes it dangerous to receive shocks out here. So far I have confined myself to little ones.
>
> (16 January 1946)

The more serious electric shocks of Gwilym's emotional life were to happen on land and in his married life.

Diaries always give away more than the keeper would wish. Gwilym's were a performance. The first I have in my possession is written in a Collins Handy Diary for 1949 and covers Gwilym's first job after qualifying as a public health inspector in Sheerness. The work presents a variety of challenges. On 20 April, Gwilym notes:

> Spent morn. trying to locate dead body causing pong at Coop Drapery Dept. They claim it is due to our poisoning – at least 12 months ago!

The body in question would have been that of a rat. In August, Gwilym has to do a 'lot of Rattus Norwegius baiting'. Gwilym doesn't have a high opinion of his clients in general. May 4 is 'Notable day for recalcitrant housing applicants – feel like taking an axe to 'em all'. August 3 is even worse, as 'umpteen viragos came and blew up about various complaints'. His attitude to women is contemptuous. On 29 June, he notes:

> Had a tricky problem today – female had bought Grade I strawberries & was convinced that they were unfit. Gave opinion that the[y] were rather ripe, but fit.

I love the muckiness of the public health inspectors' concerns. For example, on 8 August, Gwilym sees '2 lots unsound food – mites, fungus & putrefaction'.

The diary entries crack jokes and feel like dress rehearsals for letters home, with their desire to reassure and amuse. On 8 February, Gwilym describes having a cold in elaborate terms, noting that he 'sneezed & blew the old proboscis all day'. He's living in lodgings, but relations with the landlady are strained: 'Had grim do – Mrs Morbid initiates operation of psychological [warfare?]'. The situation is made happier by an instant bond between Gwilym and the landlady's dog, which he walks daily and takes swimming when the weather warms, despite an 'unpleasant experience with eels while bathing in the dark'. Soon, the dog has an operation to remove a kidney stone. However, on 14 August, Gwilym and Tony are in trouble:

> Had dog out & when we got home at 11pm [the doors] were locked. Effected entry via front room bay & felt like Bill Sykes & bull terrier.

I find a staged photograph of the dog, who clearly was important to Gwilym.

Tony, Mrs Fox's dog

Written in my father's shaky geriatric handwriting is the explanation:

> Tony Mrs Fox's dog in Sheerness. I lodged with Mrs Fox & I believe that I arranged the dog with one of my pipes & took the photograph with my ancient 'bellows' camera.

In a later pencil note, he specifies 'cherry wood pipe'.

Gwilym's luck with women is patchy. At a dance on 17 March the 'talent was very sparse & secured'. On 30 April, the women are not up to his brilliance: 'Handed down another line in vain.' In August, though, Gwilym takes a woman called Kit out and goes for a swim with Diana but on 10 September his luck improves: '*Great day … Actually managed to crash in successfully at Wheatsheaf dance.' His real feelings are expressed in Welsh: '*Dyw'r amserau'r rhyfeddodau ddim wedi ymadael a ni*' ('The time of wonders has not left us'). Gwilym begins to walk out with Mavis.

Soon after begins an even bigger love affair, when he sees a Vincent motorbike and orders one for himself. Bess, registration plate number LYT 630, takes over from the dog and Mavis in the journal. It's a symbol of his independence and being able to withdraw into his own world – a habit that changed little during the rest of Gwilym's life.

My parents met when Gwilym returned to Wales to work in the Public Health Department of Cardiff City Council. At the same time, Eryl had come to the city and was teaching in Caerphilly Girls' Grammar School at the entrance to the Rhymney valley. Tŷ'r Cymry ('House of the Welsh') was a terraced building on 11 Gordon Rd in Cardiff, just round the corner from the Mansion House, the mayor's residence, and became something of a marriage bureau for my parents' generation. Both Gwilym and Eryl threw themselves into the Welsh-language social life of the city.

Events are organised for Tuesday and Sunday evenings. In the

1956–7 year, highlights include a lecture by the Reverend D. Jacob Davies on *'Rhai o Feirdd Morgannwg'* ('Some Glamorganshire Poets'), folk dancing, under the care of Miss Elinor Williams of Barry, Mr D. Watkin Morgan discussing *'Profiad Cymro Dinesig'* ('The Urban Welshman's Experience') and, on 17 March, 'A Talk by the Reverend G. Nantlais Williams'. By virtue of his position as secretary, Gwilym had written to a Gwyn M. Daniel, thanking him for his service in the house. He responded to Gwilym's thank-you letter, noting: *'Hyfrydwch oedd ei ddarllen mewn iaith mor gain ac ysgrifen o safon aruchel'* ('It was a delight to read it in such refined language and in a hand of lofty standard').

This would have pleased Gwilym greatly. When he returned from the war, he had reinvented aspects of himself. He bought Osmiroid calligraphy pens and taught himself elegant italic script. Black ink replaced the feminine blue of his wartime self on paper. In the age of hand-written correspondence, this was a form of cultural cosmetic surgery.

Gwilym paid the same careful attention to his Welsh. In a letter sent to his father during the war, when Gwilym was in the navy, he reproached David Lewis for writing in English:

> *Diolch yn fawr am dy lythyr Dad ac am yr hanes yr trip i Benybont. Yr unig peth sy'n peri gofid imi yw y f[f]aith yr ysgrifennaist yn Saesneg. Paid byth a [g]wneud hynny eto.*
>
> (Thank you very much for your letter Dad and the tale of the trip to Bridgend. The only thing that causes me to worry is the fact that you wrote in English. Don't ever do that again.)
>
> (18 July 1945)

I'm astonished that Gwilym called his father by the familiar '*ti*' or 'thou'. My sister and I, no doubt following Eryl's Cardiganshire family, were expected to address our parents by the formal '*chi*' ('*vous*' in French). Not only were we denied the linguistic intimacy of '*ti*', along with its implication of equality between children and parents, we would never have dared to criticise their actions so directly, even in jest. For his part, David Lewis, from what I can see, took no notice of his son on this matter.

The Welsh-speaking working class in Ogmore Vale was rapidly becoming anglicised. Writing to congratulate her nephew on my birth, Gwilym's Auntie Irene (Renée) turns to Welsh in the middle of a letter in English. A theological student has tried out for the post of minister in Hermon, the family chapel:

> *Ofnaf mae'n rhy dda i ddod yma. Mae'n siwr i gael galwad yn well na hwn. Yng Coleg Aberystwyth mae e yn awr.* [I fear he's too good to come here. He's bound to get a better call than this. He's in Aberystwyth College now.]
>
> How's that for a spot of Cymraeg [Welsh]. Miss S. J. Hughes called with Urdd [a Welsh-language youth organisation] flags the week before last. We carried on quite a conversation. A word of English almost makes her shudder. She's the complete Welsh crank.

Gwilym made a stand and went against the family's grain in this matter. While not an overt nationalist, he took a course in Welsh orthography and secured his grip on Welsh grammar. Eryl and I relied on instinct to tell us when our mutations – the hardest part of learning Welsh – were correct, but Gwilym knew the rules. Friends in Ceredigion still comment on the polish of my father's clean Welsh, meaning that he didn't use English words instead of those for which Welsh already existed.

As part of his self-improvement, Gwilym kept a book of Welsh vocabulary, which I used as the basis of an elegy for him in my last collection of poems in Welsh. I found it distressing that Gwilym would turn to English with me in the last months of his life. This elegy is written in English (shocking in a Welsh book), dramatising the disappearance of my parents' rich idioms. Here, in a poem called '*Llyfr Geirfa fy Nhad*' ('My Father's Vocabulary Book'), I juxtapose Gwilym's learning of words with his forgetting them. I translate the Welsh in the body of the poem:

What was he reading
Bron bob gyda'r nos – almost every night?

He was *wrth fy modd* –
at his pleasure – learning that *rhawn*
was horsehair. As for his soul
ar ddifancoll – lost in perdition? Swearing
was By Goblin – *Myn coblyn* and prissy lout

llabwst. My father's Welsh
was Biblical, so, when he was dying

and asked me, '*Beth yw gwelltog?*'
We felt the shadow of the valley of death.
Gwelltog is green, as in pastures, lie down.

Gwilym Lewis was as meticulous in his record-keeping as Ben James. At his retirement party, thrown by the Cardiff City Council Environmental Health Department, a colleague recalled being trained by my father. Having inspected a ship together one morning, they returned to the office and, settling himself down at his desk, Gwilym lit his pipe and then pronounced that: 'We do expenses first, and all else follows'. Long after he'd stopped driving in old age, I found a notebook he kept, logging the mileage per gallon of petrol for every car he'd owned since the late 1970s. At the end of his life, this mania for details led him to note the date on batteries he inserted into smoke detectors or quartz clocks so that, when he changed them, he could gauge which brands performed best.

He was also a hoarder of text (I suffer from the same affliction). I like the attention to detail it shows but lament its lack of perspective. Part of judgement is being able to distinguish the precious from the surrounding noise. Because I'm dissenting from the family version of our story, these hoarding tendencies have given me a paper trail to follow for evidence.

—This isn't a court of law, you know. You don't need to prove everything.
—I don't trust myself at all.
—How you feel now is all you need to know.
—I doubt myself so much that I need confirmation of my own story.
—I believe you, Gwyn, and I always will.
—Who did you say you were again?

Once my parents married, the paper trail becomes more impersonal. Eryl takes over record-keeping and starts the 106 Heol Gabriel House Log Book, which has a black, glossy cover. From February 1958 onward, it's a record of housekeeping, rather than personal matters. Expenditure on food is logged for each day – the list has the plainness of wartime rationing: cheese, bread, baked beans, filet of lamb, oranges. On 2 February 1958 the beech hedge goes into the front garden of Eryl and Gwilym's Wimpy semi-detached house on a new estate in Whitchurch. Dad had visited the site regularly to keep an eye on the building, knocking out concrete from the drains. He found out later that he'd been caring for the wrong house.

The opening page, for the week ending 8 February, shows that Eryl makes twenty-one pounds of marmalade in January and that then, on the thirtieth, the washing machine is oiled. Oiling the washing machine is a frequent ritual, undertaken with the fervour of one who'd been brought up to wash everything with a washboard, mangle and a solid iron that had to be warmed by the fire and carefully cleaned before pressing clothes. We use them now as door stops. Such was Eryl's dread of being unable to wash, that she took out a special insurance policy on the machine till the end of her life.

The detail in the entries surprises me. For example, Eryl notes that she bought a feather quilt in David Morgan's in the January 1959 sale for £5-6-0 ('reduced from £8-19-6 to £6-6-0, and £1 allowed as I did not buy set'). On 14 August 1959 they 'swept dining room chimney – moderate amount of soot.' Not a lot, just some. Clearly, Eryl has an eagle eye. There was no question of paying a chimneysweep to do the job; Gwilym buys his own set of brushes, with brass-tipped sections that screw together to lengthen the brush. I remember he used to store them in the outside toilet.

The first hint in the house log that Eryl's pregnant is an entry on 15 August:

> Bought Kestos nursing bra at D. Morgans (15/11 – 34")
> Separate pads are 2/3 <u>each</u> – not bought yet.

In the underlining of 'each' I can hear in Mam's voice that she thinks the pads are scandalously expensive. Perhaps the weekly budget didn't allow for buying everything at once. Or maybe there was a caution there: no need to spend more than she had to before the pregnancy was closer to full term.

There's nesting going on, with curtains being cleaned, Venetian blinds arriving and a nylon shawl being knitted. On 24 August Eryl oils the washing machine again and bottles plums. By 9 September, she's ready to buy a baby bath: 'Jury, Double Brand Homeware, made from Rigidex' and also a bin:

> Laricol product.– guaranteed for 3 yrs. under all normal conditions. Do <u>not</u> bring into contact with hot surfaces or near a naked flame.

I'm not surprised by how meticulously my parents looked after their possessions. No doubt this was a result of wartime austerity and the frugality needed to live within their means. In the future, some of the most vicious reprimands I'm given are to do with my damaging objects. I'm a dropper of the breakable, a spiller of liquids. Once I accidentally tipped nail-varnish remover over my parents' Ercol table, and was never allowed to forget it.

At the end of October wallflowers are planted, lavender bags made and, on the twenty-first, Mam 'Finished Quickerknit Baby Shawl – very little left out of the 16oz'. With the baby's arrival imminent, the washing machine is oiled again and, on 3 November, 'painless contractions' have begun. By the following day, Eryl's admitted to the Northlands Salvation Army nursing home.

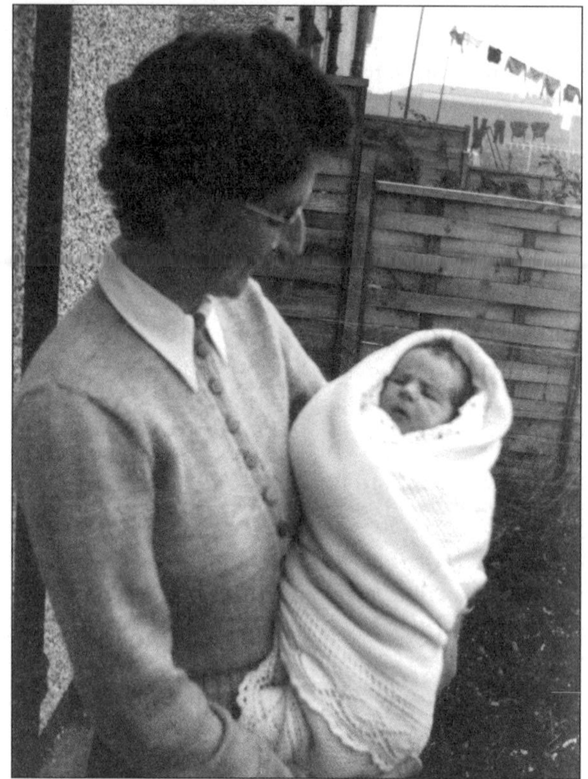

Eryl and newborn Gwyneth, November 1959

On 4 November 1959 I arrive:

> Gwyneth born 4.35 p.m. Delivered by Major Singleton; 7lbs. 2 oz.

Eryl kept every single greeting card and letter sent to her on my birth. The sheer number shows how many friends my parents had at this stage of their lives. By the time they retired, this circle had dwindled to one or two exceptions. The line immediately underneath my weight notes: 'See page 61 for gifts received'. It's two pages long and includes a beloved toy dog made of white rabbit skin, with black button eyes and a red felt tongue given by Eryl's godmother. For some reason obscure to me, my parents don't bother appointing godparents for me or my sister.

Personalised greetings came from Eryl's former pupils in the sixth form at Caerphilly Grammar School, who sent flowers to the nursing home and enclosed a poem 'To Mrs Lewis', who was obviously a popular teacher:

> To the nicest English mistress
> And her lucky hubby, too,
> We would like to send these wishes
> For both your lives right through.
> May good fortune smile upon you
> In the best way we can tell
> And may you not forget us,
> (Last year's fifth you loved so well)
> For we all are thinking of you:
> From these solid desks of ours,
> From our lessons, lunch-breaks, intervals,
> And even from our showers.

Ben and Sarah Ann sent a card showing a Silver Cross Pram on the outside. Open the card and a combination of baby carriage and Holy Spirit delivers a pop-out infant sitting up and grinning. The greeting is plain: 'Congratulations and Best Wishes to You All, Mam & Dat' in Ben James's hand. In a few months' time, I'm sitting up in my own pram, posing for the camera.

Several of the notes sent to congratulate Eryl show that her friends know of her resentment towards her sister Megan. By now, she and Bill in America have five sons. My Great Auntie Muriel writes:

> I do hope that all is going on as well as possible with you Eryl and the little daughter, just what you wanted Eryl. Your sister will be quite envious of you.
>
> (6 November 1959)

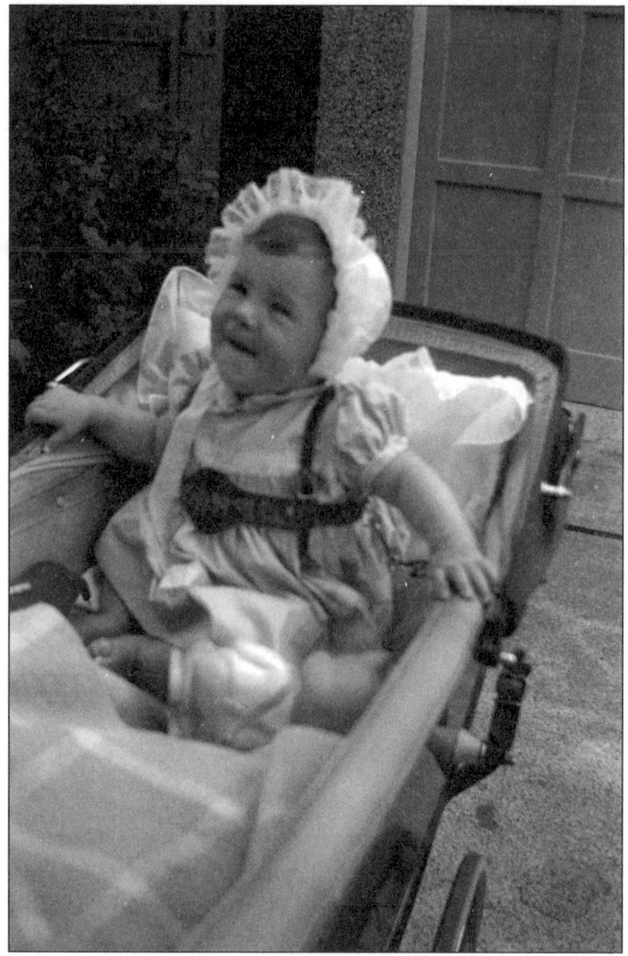

Gwyneth

Eve, a friend from Pengam, joins in: 'It's lovely that you were able to produce a little girl – hope your sister won't be too envious!!' A friend whose name I don't recognise but who Eryl had clearly told about her upbringing speculates:

> I wonder what they think [in] America!! At least they can have the satisfaction of having a niece! I always

> remember your remark from the heart, I'm sure – about at last achieving something Megan hadn't managed.
>
> (5 November 1959)

Eryl's godmother, who really knew the dynamic between the sisters, confirms that she may have scored a rare victory over Megan:

> So you have beaten Megan in having a daughter first. I am sure she will be delighted; but I am afraid the Tanner boys were hoping for another boy to add to the family. They don't seem to like girls very much.

Reading a note from Margaret Regan, a teaching colleague and friend from Eryl's first school, sends a chill through my heart. Eryl has clearly confided in her older colleague about her isolation at home:

> Now that G. has arrived you'll have plenty of company & plenty to do so you won't need cheering up ~~so much~~ so I shan't haunt you so much in the future, but I'll call one of these days fairly soon to see G.

This is the first sign I can see on paper of the shadows to come. If cheering up Eryl was my purpose in life, then I made things far worse.

—*That was never your job.*
—*So I didn't fail?*
—*What ailed Eryl was already there. You were born into a trap.*

Chapter 3
DAMNATION

Pa sawl math o blant sydd?
Dau fath.
Pa rai yw'r ddau fath?
Plant da, a phlant drwg …
Beth yw dyletswydd plant tuag at eu rhieni?
Eu caru ac ufuddhau iddynt.

(*Rhodd Mam*)

(How many kinds of children are there?
Two kinds.
What are the two kinds?
Good children and bad children …
What is children's duty towards their parents?
To love and obey them.)

(*Mother's Gift*)

Rage transforms my mother into a bird. Eryl's face turns grey, the eyes widen, her nose becomes hawk-like. Her lips disappear and, as she works herself up further, her mouth tightens into a circle, with wrinkles stitching it into place. I think of it as a hen's asshole, even though I've never seen one up close. She's reluctant to smack but, when riled enough, takes me and my sister by the shoulders and shakes us, so that the world becomes blurred, detached from the brainstem. Marian and I agree that we quite like the feeling.

I'm five or six and am sitting in the porch of my parents' house, taking off antique roller skates. My sister's are shop-bought, with four rubber-covered wheels and red leather ties at the toes and heel. My vintage pair, which belonged to my father as a child, has metal clamps which have to be adjusted with a key to grip my shoes at the toes. The wheels are ball-bearings (no tyres) and the metal leaves white streaks, like figure-skating scars on the pavement's ice. The whole street can hear me pounding down the hill, over the cul-de-sac entrance and down to our front gate. I hate this noise but skate as elegantly as I can, in the hope that a promoter in a passing Rolls-Royce sees my artistic genius and Takes Me Away From All This. Cars are scarce enough in the late 1960s on Heol Gabriel that, on particularly boring afternoons, we collect registration numbers.

Next to me on the porch step is the family order of milk, delivered in glass bottles. As I tussle with the cracked leather strap my right elbow jerks back and catches one of them. It shatters. I watch in horror as the milk spreads. A liquid peninsula reaches my bottom and soaks into my brown nylon slacks. The flood raises itself over the lip of the doorstep, overflows onto the concrete approach to the house. Shards of milky glass stick up like jagged teeth in red gums.

Picking up the largest pieces of fragments and putting them in the bin, I decide to go for the cover-up. Frantic, I find a rag in the outside toilet and try to mop up the milk. The smaller shards of glass scrape against the tiles, a sensation that goes through me. I can't make the porch look clean and dry. I run to my friends, Madelaine, Julie and Elaine, and beg them to ask their mothers if they can lend me a spare pint, I'll pay them. Nobody takes mercy on me.

Eryl's fury goes from nought to sixty in a second and follows a set pattern. First, the interrogation: every detail of my crime is extracted from me and examined. She does not recognise the idea of an accident. Any misdemeanour is a deliberate act of disobedience directed personally at her. I am a clumsy clot. Why didn't I take more care? Don't I know how dangerous it is to touch broken glass? What if I'd cut myself? How dare I try to cover up what happened? I've shown Mam up in front of the neighbours. What must Mrs Jenkins, Mrs Cronin, Mrs Dart think? I'm a liar, she's ashamed of me. She ruminates on every aspect of my error and magnifies it, element by element. Once she reaches a certain pitch of exasperation with me, she screams:

'Get out of my sight!'

This phrase comes back to me decades later, when I'm blinded by migraine, and I wonder if the world has banished me from its sight once and for all.

I flee to my bedroom. Even upstairs, though, I'm not safe. Every time her anger rises to a certain pitch again, Eryl bursts through the door and has another jab at me, like a dog tearing at a carcass. I know that she'll be back. Loud noises have always frightened me, a result, no doubt, of having the migraineur's over-excitable brain. The shouting lands on me like blows, words used as blunt instruments around the head. I'm cornered and, so, have to listen to the assaulting words. I experience these attacks as verbal beatings.

Even more damaging is being wiped out as a person. My explanations simply provoke more outrage. Eryl's the one who's been hurt, so I count for nothing. My sense of self – of having good reasons for doing things, of making moral choices, even if they're the wrong ones – is blotted out.

If your mother tells you often during your early childhood that you're wicked, you believe her. But another part of me also knows that this treatment's unjust. My opinion of myself splits in two. So starts the double moral vision about myself that gives me emotional vertigo to this day.

Compared to being shouted at, being banished to my bedroom is, initially, a relief. My childhood room's above the garage, so is chilly.

I look out of the window, to watch the neighbours coming and going. We live in a Wimpey estate in Whitchurch, a Cardiff suburb. I rest my elbows on the windowsill, chin in my hands. It becomes a kind of meditation. There's a young woman opposite whose hair, gathered in a ponytail, hangs down to her waist, so I have a crush on her. I'm told that she works in a bank, which seems exotic to me. Up the street is Sable the Alsatian dog, who once licked my face so thoroughly that I came home to say that Sable had 'washed me' – to my mind, a great blessing.

Cardiff is built in a coastal crater, surrounded on three sides by a ring of high ground. From my window, I can see the Wenallt and the three masts on Caerphilly Mountain. What I think I can see is Golgotha, Christ's cross in the middle of the two thieves. Dacu had given me a metal crucifix about six inches high on a stand, and I keep it in my room.

At dusk one evening, I hear the uncanny yowling of two cats in a stand-off. The raw aggression makes me think that a baby is being murdered. I locate one cat, sat on a windowsill, its profile like an owl. I am that creature out in the dark, but wanting to sit next to the fire inside. I can hear family life happening downstairs without me. I wrap myself in the eiderdown with its cover pattern of green fishing vessels, and cry till someone comes and forgives me and life is possible again.

The best clue I have now about how ostracisation feels for a child is the recurring nightmares I still experience as an adult. I've fallen out of favour with the person I love most in the world and without whom I can't survive (their identity varies but the effect is always the same). The figure can be male, but the intensity of the emotions suggests that it's a maternal drama. I know that this person has loved me passionately but something I've done, of which they don't approve, means that the warm yellow beam of light, in which I've been happier than I ever have been, is suddenly switched off and applied to somebody else. The jealousy and outrage are intense. My existence is at stake and I'm hyperventilating with dread. In the dream, I accept fully that I no longer deserve this person's love but I'm at a complete loss about how to regain it. This task is even harder because I never really understand what I've done wrong, but I'm convinced, nevertheless, that I'm guilty. I search, beg, plead and pray, but that golden attention has been definitively withdrawn because of my own actions and it's all my fault. This is the despair of the damned: you had it all and blew it.

Living without that love is unbearable.

Our chapel is Calvinistic Methodists and so belongs to 'Yr Hen Gorff' ('The Old Body'), as opposed to the softer Wesleyans. Presumably, therefore, we believe in predestination, but it's never mentioned. This is a curious omission. I learn about the difference between salvation by faith, rather than works, from history lessons in school but not from chapel, which would have been the logical place for such an education. In principle, the whole drama of salvation and damnation is decided before we're born. It's possible, therefore, for a criminal with faith to enter heaven and for a person whose life was full of good deeds but no faith to be damned. As a student, I'm thrilled to discover James Hogg's *The Private Memoirs and Confessions of a Justified Sinner*, published in 1824, a novel taking this position to its logical and Gothic extreme. The sinner of the title is among God's Elect before the start of time, using the theological immunity from damnation this affords him to pursue a life of depravity. Is this doctrine an embarrassing secret from our denomination's past? Do we no longer believe in it? We should have been told.

At home, my own drama of predestination is being played out, with Eryl as an unpredictable God. Her unconscious identification of me with her own sister means that I have been set up for condemnation. I'm nearly four years old in September 1963, when Eryl writes a letter to Gwilym, who's in Eastbourne for a public health conference. She has been looking after Julie, a neighbour's child the same age as me:

Annwyl Gwilym,

Gair ar frys tra mae M. yn cysgu a G. yn gwylio 'Bill & Ben'. Mae G mewn 'disgrace' *bore 'ma am iddi hi a Julie ysgwyd tin o dalcum powder ar hyd y room ffrynt* – mes[s] *ofnadwy a fi newydd lanhau'r ystafell.*

Mae'r merched yn falch iawn o gael eich cardiau – G. wrth gwrs am gael yr un arall bob tro yn lle ei un ei hunan.

(Dear Gwilym,

A quick word while M. is sleeping and G. watching 'Bill & Ben'. G. is in disgrace this morning because she and Julie shook a tin of talcum powder over the front room – a terrible mess and I'd just cleaned it.

The girls are very pleased to receive your cards – G. of course wanting to have the other one every time instead of her own.)

No sooner am I mentioned than I'm in the wrong. Eryl used to say that I loved watching television so much that she thought that I wasn't very bright. Marian manages to please my parents hugely when, just learning to write in English, she chalks a sweet message on her infant blackboard:

For Dad and Mam I will do Enithin

This is a charming expression of gratitude and must have touched my parents deeply. With my rebellious heart, I could never have written this, not even in childhood. I know already that this statement is giving too much away. Nobody has the right to expect everything from somebody else, especially not parents of a child. A child should do what's right for herself – within the general limits of socialisation – and know that, whatever that is, it's fine. Gwilym and Eryl, naturally, treasure my sister's message and keep it propped up by the garage door, where it sits until after their deaths. Every time I pass the sign, I dissent inwardly and feel reproached.

It's not that I'm ungrateful for my parents' care. Aged five or six, in primary school, when my grip on grammar is still very shaky and my spelling flamboyant, I write to thank Eryl for making a wickerwork cradle for my doll:

> *Yr wi yn caru chi yn fawr iawn gambo chi wedi gwneid Llawer o Pethau Caredeg. Yche chi yn hoffu Pethau lliwgar … Pwu liw chi yn hoffi gorau[.] w'i yn hoffu pengc orau[.] Pwu lun chi yn hoffu gorai[.] w'i yn hoffu y Rheban. oddiwrth GwyNeth*
> *erel Lewis i mam Heiol Gebriyj 106 Welchsh […] Glarmogyn Caerdudd Cymru Brechesh eels ewrop the wyld*
> *xxxxxxx XXXXXXXxxxxx*

> (Ai love you very much becoz you have done Many Kind Things. Do you like colourful Things … Wat colour you like best[.] i leic pengc [pink] best[.] Wat picture you leic best[.] I leick the Rebbon. from GwyNeth
> erel Lewis to mam Heiol Gebriyj 106 Welchsh […] Glarmogyn Cardyff Wales Brechesh eels ewrop the wyld
> xxxxxxx XXXXXXXxxxxx)

See? I was capable of being a loving child and was always grateful. But, compared to my sister at the same age, I hold back. My feelings are deeply mixed. I find a card I made for Eryl. On the front is an unusual blue Christmas pudding with holly antlers on top drawn in wax crayon. The message inside is the reserved:

> *Annwyl Mam*
> *Wyi yn lecio*
> *chi. i Mam*
> *oddi wrth Gwyneth*

> Dear Mam
> Ai leik
> you. to Mam
> from Gwyneth

The photographs of our early years show that there were happy times. When I was an infant, Gwilym had the knack of reducing me to helpless laughter. In several photos he tickles me, laughing above me like a tree. Our favourite picture, though, shows me on my own and was taken by Gwilym with his Kodak box camera. We were on our way to Llanddewi Brefi to see my grandparents and had stopped on a Cambrian Mountain road, no doubt for the relief of bladders. I'm about three, with short hair and wearing a red gingham dress under a fully buttoned home-made cardigan, so it must have been chilly. On my feet is a pair of hated brown lace-up Start-Rite shoes for the correction of knock knees. Gwilym said later that he had no idea what had amused me, but:

'*Dyna'r llun gore dynnes i erioed.*'

('That's the best picture I ever took.')

These were the times of salvation. On Sunday mornings, our special treat was to get into our parents' G-plan double bed for a *cwtsh* ('cuddle'). After some snuggling and talking, Dad would always get up first and, as he sat on the side of the bed in his pyjama bottoms, Eryl would run her hand, loose and relaxed, up and down his back until she'd teased shivers of goosebumps over his skin. We demanded this show of frisson every time, but she didn't always oblige. These are the ordinary miracles of family contentment: the smell of Eryl's hair as she kissed me good night. Her upper arm against my cheek as she read stories to us, our backs to the storage heater. If she was in a particularly good mood, she'd waggle her ears, which produced admiration and mirth in us girls.

Eryl took infinite trouble to make sure that we were healthy, well nourished and beautifully clothed. We had all the books that we needed and many more, plus all the encouragement and help to do well in education. I could read before I went to school and learned quickly to write. If anything, too much attention was the problem.

Gwyneth laughing

While we're at primary school, our class is invited to take part in a Cymanfa Ganu for children at Capel Tabernacl in the Hayes. During the Methodist revival, Nonconformists devised the Cymanfa, a singing festival, as a special treat. It's a revival meeting but without readings or sermons and consists only of hymns – a religious karaoke festival. The Codwr Canu ('Song Raiser' or conductor), usually a charismatic figure, well known to the local congregation, rehearses the singers into their separate voices, before putting it all together in a rousing four-part harmony. If it goes particularly well, we're forced to sing the hymn again. When anybody demands that I feel pious and emotional, something shuts off in my heart. Cold and unsmiling, I look at him (and in those days, it was always a man) resentfully, willing the whole occasion to be over as soon as possible. Maybe this is why Eryl hates chapel. She has a point.

At school, we spend weeks beforehand copying out the lyrics of the songs into a Glamorgan Education Committee exercise book which I still have. Choruses are depicted with squiggles like snake tracks between each verse. As a break from religion – or perhaps a sidelight on sin – one of the songs is about a gamekeeper, whose job is to prevent poaching on a rural estate. Reading it now, it's an intriguing lyric about the balance of power between law breaker and enforcer, the miscreant and God:

1. Y cipar aeth i hela'n hy
Ymysg y llwyni gwyrddion.

(1. The keeper boldly went to hunt
Among the green bushes.)

This is a very strange hunt, though, because the various poachers on the estate run rings around the keeper:

2. Y cyntaf un, ei fethu a wnaeth,
Ymysg y llwyni gwyrddion.
3. Yr ail hyd ato am gusan a ddaeth,
Ymysg y llwyni gwyrddion.
4. Y trydydd i ffwrdd i rhywle a aeth
Ymysg y llwyni gwyrddion.

(2. The first, he failed to catch,
Among the green bushes.
3. The second came to him for a kiss,
Among the green bushes.
4. The third away to somewhere went
Among the green bushes.)

The hunted both hate and love the gamekeeper; it's a situation of mutual bafflement. In the end, he ends up an isolated and impotent figure in the woods. There's a second etymology of the name 'Eryl' than the one that links her to Crugeryr. Dating from the fourteenth century, the feminine noun means 'a hunt, chase, pursuit'. But 'Eryl, erhyl' is one of that strange subgroup of words which also mean its opposite: to 'watch, guard; order, method' and 'assault'. This contronym sums up my confusion about my Eryl. This has only grown, not lessened, with the passing of time.

Our class has been placed in the front row of the chapel gallery, giving me an excellent view of the parents below – Eryl among them – and of the hated conductor in full control of the crowd and, therefore, in his oils. I'm bored out of my mind, lean over the edge and – disaster! – lose hold of my pamphlet, which flutters down, like a white butterfly, to the red carpet below. I run downstairs and retrieve my book. Eryl has noticed what happened and I know what's ahead of me.

When we get home, I'm told that I've made a show of myself. I'm accused of being careless, of doing it deliberately. Who do I think I am? Banishment awaits. As a child, I have nowhere to escape Eryl-as-hunter.

Now that I'm a mature adult and Eryl's dead, the balance of power is reversed. I worry that I'm hunting my own mother in this book, and she with no chance of defending herself. I can never feel wholly right about this, but it's a question of choosing between two wrongs.

—Don't crumble now. It's not a virtue.

—My sister thinks I've done a poison pen job on Eryl, that I've only remembered the bad things.

—And Leighton?

—He says I've been far too soft on her.

—That sounds about right then.

—But how dare *I?*

—That's Eryl's voice in your head. Ignore it.

—What if I'm committing a terrible injustice?

—You're not. Just write this well and all will come good.

Like Mam's rages, the Reverend Lodwig Jones's sermons take a set form. He wears his grey hair in a quiff, shaped to an intriguing wave at the front, and is an old-style fire and brimstone preacher. He starts in a relaxed key, quoting the piece of Scripture that shows the ideal demonstrated by Christ. Then, with infinite sadness, he outlines our moral failings compared with what the Bible requires. Then he becomes very angry with us, then full of despair. Finally, the voice of doom modulates into an awed contemplation of God's grace. This last section requires much slower speech and words weighed, like coins, in his right hand (held alongside the pocket watch in his waistcoat) as he draws to his ponderous conclusion. This emotional wash cycle always takes at least forty minutes to complete. It's considered too long for the children to bear, so we're sent down to the vestry to be amused by various Bible-related activities, unless you jib completely, being too young or too clingy to leave your parent. Then the time can be passed by counting the pipes on the organ or the number of hats in the congregation. I remember falling asleep using my father's bony thigh as a pillow.

Before being allowed down to the vestry in the morning, the children have to go to the *Sedd Fawr* ('the Big Seat'), where the deacons sit. We face the congregation and recite a chosen *adnod* (verse). This is nerve-racking. '*Duw cariad yw*' ('God is love') and '*Myfi yw bara'r bywyd*' ('I am the bread of life') are good, short stand-bys, but can only be used by infants. Older children are expected to learn longer sections, like the Beatitudes ('Blessed are the pure of heart'), etc. During the week, we have to memorise and practise the verses. My father writes them on a strip of paper, which he slips into his glasses case so that, if we forget our words, he can prompt us. When we're in our teens, a friend who's a poet begins to improvise verses, and is such a clever mimic that few people notice. Gwilym, whose grandfather was a Methodist minister, is perhaps more alert to this than many and relishes these performances.

In Sunday school, with Mrs Jenkins, we're always making models of Holy Land scenes, like the house from which a paralytic in the Gospel was hoisted out through the roof by his friends, in order to be healed by Jesus. We glue actual pebbles and sand to the model with my favourite adhesive, Bostik. This comes in an orange tube not unlike an epi-pen. I love spreading it over my fingers, allowing it to dry and then peeling it off, like sunburned skin. Now, every time I apply for a visa to work in the United States, the person fingerprinting me complains that I have practically no identifying ridges on the tips of my fingers. The Vestry Bostik took them.

Sunday is always a danger day in terms of Eryl's moods. When both my sister and I were in school full-time, she had returned to teaching, so fatigue from the week and the need to prepare lessons for Monday meant that she needed time to herself. She never pretended to believe in God. Her keen critical sense would have made her impatient with the old-fashioned verbosity and sexism of Calvinistic Methodism. She felt little love for men of the cloth. Gwilym takes us to Roath Park Lake after Sunday school and we feed the ducks with stale bread, which we now know is entirely the wrong diet. (The current recommendation is frozen peas.) We're dressed in our Sunday best: matching dresses for me and my sister, black patent-leather shoes and sagging white tights that don't quite reach my crotch and, so, make me feel like a penguin.

> To speak is to feed. To speak is to suck the breast of the common logical mother. The word is born of this mother, always a virgin, since she is always intact, somewhere, since the language always exceeds my command of it … I feed myself endlessly at the buffet of my language: I shall never be able to give it what it gave me. I am the noise of its complicated harmony, or its wail. I would die from not writing; I would die of not taking my feast of words with a few friends, from whom, somehow, I get my language. I shall never be weaned from it.
>
> (Michel Serres)

Once I learn to write, I can begin to feed myself with my own version of reality. I'm about six when I write a long letter to my grandparents recounting one of my scrapes. I tell them that Mam and I had been to the cinema to see *The Ugly Dachshund* which, in my opinion '*oedd yn itha twp*' ('was quite stupid') and *Tender-foot*, a film in which, I write, '*o ni bron a cruo achos yr oedd inidan cochuon yn ymladd a soldieors*' ('I nearly craied because Rad Induans were fighting with soldieors'). In Winnie the Pooh '*oedd rabit wedi rhoi pethau ar pen ôl winnie the Pooh*' ('rabit had put things on winnie the Pooh's bottom'). Eryl had unpicked the seams of an old skirt of hers with a blue lattice pattern on it and made me a very attractive sundress:

> *ar ddydd Gwener dyna fi a marian yn mynd i'r cae a dyna ffrind marian yn galw arnon ni i ddod i warae* fish and chip shop. *a oedd yn rhi bell i gerdded i tŷ ffrind marian. so oedd rhoid i ni dringo dros y ffens a chi'n gweld oedd marian felu drengo dros y ffens a oedd fi wedi dringo dros y ffens a wedyn dyna fi yn cwnpo dros y ffens –*
>
> (on Friday me and marian went to the field and marian's friend called us to come and pley fish and chip shop. and it was too fare to walk to marian's friend's house. so we haves to climb over the fence and you see marian cants climb over the fence and I have climb over the fence and then I fells over the fence –)

And there the letter stops abruptly, the following pages lost. Clearly, I'm too lazy to walk the long way round and I try to implicate my sister in my actions. I remember everything: the diamond-shaped wire fence, echoing the blue lattice pattern in the fabric of my new dress; getting stuck at the top and, unable to regulate my fall, toppling to the ripping sound of material. The dress is ruined and I face knives at home again. But Ben James's response is measured:

> *Diolch yn fawr am eich llythyr da. Yr wyf yn gweld eich bod yn dysgu yn dda iawn yn yr ysgol … Trueni ofnadwy i chwi rwygo eich ffrog newydd sbon.*

> *Mwnciod sydd yn hoffi dringo. Yr oedd yn dda nad oeddech chi wedi aros ar y ffens. Feallai bod mam wedi gwneud yr un peth pan oedd yn fach.*
>
> (Thank you very much for your good letter. I see that you're learning well in school … It's a terrible pity that you ripped your brand-new dress. It's monkeys that like to climb. It was good that you didn't stay on the fence. Perhaps mam did the same thing when she was little.)

When I discover this letter recently, I'm overjoyed to see my grandfather defending me from Eryl's ire. He then goes on to tell me about the cats that visit their garden, drawing a picture of two running away from him. I also love that he's more interested in the quality of my writing than in my being a model child.

No wonder I was always longing to be in Llanddewi Brefi. On the latest visit to my grandparents, I'd played with Morfudd, the golden-headed daughter of Peggy, the postwoman in Tregaron, and fallen in love. Back in Cardiff, eighty-four miles away, Eryl sees me haring up the hill toward the Philog. At the top, she catches up with me and asks to know where I'm going. It seems obvious to me:

'To see Morfudd!'

Emotionally, I'm off. At various times, I fantasise about running away to live in the Nazareth House orphanage on North Road. In my ignorance, I imagine it as a version of Enid Blyton's Malory Towers. I also have my eye on the lighthouse on Roath Park Lake.

Compared to Methodist hymns, the catches and songs I learn with my English-speaking friends are much more earthy. We're the only Welsh-speaking family in Heol Gabriel, aside from the Joneses and their two young sons up the road. I remember standing next to Elaine, who lives three doors down from us in Whitchurch, and beginning to play with a gang of her friends, even though I can't understand what they're saying but that doesn't last long. If you speak two languages, they don't exist in watertight compartments. Sounds and meanings leak into each other, within each language and between both. My first attempts at writing in English are spelt the Welsh way: 'Ddy cat sat on ddy mat'. When we play 'Cowboys and Indians', the word 'injured' means something associated with Native Americans because they were 'Injuns'. At the same age, when I go to a Christmas party held for council workers' children at Cardiff's City Hall, I don't know the words to *Rudolph the Red-Nosed Reindeer*.

On the street, we play a clapping game to words which described a romantic relationship:

My boyfriend's name is Fatty,
He comes from Cincinnati,
With a pimple on his nose
And three black toes,
And this is how my story goes.

One day when I was walking,
I saw my boyfriend talking
To a pretty little girl
With one black curl
And this is what he said to her:

'I love you, oh so dearly
And someone else sincerely'.
So he jumped in a lake
And swallowed a snake
And came back up with a belly ache.

Another jingle is even more basic. This is recited with an inverted crossing of the self, by touching both nipples, then gesturing towards urethra and bottom:

Milk, milk, lemonade,
Chocolate round the corner.

Lewis family, c.1963

The animal happiness of children is experienced in the belly and bowels. I still recall the sagging in my pants when I've pooed myself into a nappy or rompers. I imagine my turds as soft rocks that mustn't be sat on or they'll explode into filth. Much better to keep waddling and ask for help. I still dream about the horror of those miniature school toilets, shit spilling out of the overflowing toilet bowl, like cruel words from a mouth.

One day, we're playing in the garage and I pull down my knickers and show the gathered company my bottom. I'm most disappointed when nobody else returns the favour. Someone tells on me. Disgrace.

In themselves, these incidents of transgression are trivial, but I experience Eryl's reaction to them as extreme, even for those more disciplinarian times. I don't remember my sister being in hot water anything like as often. The pattern of mischief followed by severe reprimand is thin as filigree to begin but, traced over, deepens, thickens into a track. Positions harden. Repetition fosters expectation, a sense of injustice incites secret rebellion. All these incidents, however light, contribute to making a way that is hard-wired in the brain and, in the future, becomes impossible to avoid.

Aged three, I begin attending a Welsh-language nursery school. At five, I graduate to Heol Llanishen Fach, which is part of expanding Welsh-language education in Cardiff. Our classes form a Welsh-language unit in the English-speaking school. We don't mix with the English-speaking children on the same site.

I have bowel problems even as I'm learning to write and keep a diary, which may not be a coincidence. The first diary I keep, aged six or seven, is an account of a Whitsun holiday which, far from being private, is explicitly written for my school mates. This journal is dedicated to them and so is a public document:

> *Annwyl blant,*
> *rwyf yn gobeithio eich bod wedi mwynhai ei gwyliau eich hyn yr un faint ac yr wyf. Ac hefyd rwyw [sic] yn*

gobeithi[o] eich bod wedi mwynhai y llyfr yma. Oddi wrth Gwyneth L.

(Dear children,
I hope that you enjoyed your own holiday as much as I have. And also I hope that you have enjoyed this book. From Gwyneth L.)

The words are in pencil, printed carefully. Writing is still a new skill, imperfectly mastered and far from being habitual. I write only in Welsh, which is a phonetic language – that is, spelt the way it's spoken – though, at this age, my orthography is enterprising. There's a formal tone to the narrative due, perhaps, to my efforts to sound 'correct'. On 27 May, my sister and I begin our holiday, but I refer to us in the third person, as if I'm confused about whether this is a diary or a short story:

Ar ôl codi cawsant frecwas blasis iawn. Cawsant gig moch a bobi dau ddarn o dost a mêl arno.

(After getting up they had a very tastie breakfas. They had bacon and two each slices of toast and honey on it.)

Like all children, I'm intensely interested in food, and praise the '*te neis neis*' ('the nice nice tea') we have after Gwilym and I had been to post a letter together. There's also an element of flattering Eryl. Children have no privacy and, therefore, assume that everything they write will be read by adults. Entries (and omissions) are made defensively, to give the minimum of incriminating evidence to a hostile reader. My sister once made the mistake of writing in her diary that, while my parents were out, we'd played with matches. Mam read the entry and so we were punished. I knew from the beginning of my writing life that I need to censor myself or to convey private matters in code. Later, I had to use French, which neither of my parents understood, to hide dangerous topics. When I went to study in England, I kept my diary in Welsh, to throw the monoglot English-language reader off the scent.

The diary also provides important evidence of events whose significance I don't understand at the time of writing. After a visit to my cousins in Gloucester, on Friday, 2 June we're back in Wales:

> *Pan gawsant frecwast y bore yma dyna dadi yn dweud 'brysiu mae'n rhaid i ti weld Docdor Jecwps y bore yma!'*
>
> (When they had breakfast this morning, dadi said 'hurry, you have to see Docdor Jecwps this morning!')

It sounds as if I'd been to see this doctor before at Cardiff's Royal Infirmary and I see it as a happy opportunity to have a long chat with my father. The Lewis side can talk for Wales. Anti Enid said that their father once went for a walk and was away for hours, but the family wasn't worried because he could 'talk to a postbox':

> *A chyn bod hir roedd dad a fi yn y car ac yn siarad tu-gulydd am y traeth.*
>
> (And before long Dad and me were in the car and talking tugether about the beach.)

I take the appointment with Dr Jacobs in my stride.

> *Ar ôl cyrraedd yr* hospital *a siarad gyda Docdor Jecyps, dyna ni yn cerdded yn ôl i'r car yn gyflym.*
>
> (After reaching the hospital and talking with Docdor Jecyps, we walked quickly back to the car.)

The reason for the visit to Dr Jacobs is that I've become constipated and had developed an anal fissure. With a child's animism, I believe that my poo is alive. I address turds as they plop into the pan and then, before flushing, saying, formally:

'Goodbye Mr Poo. Goodbye Mrs Poo.'

I love them dearly and feel sad that they're leaving. So far, so Freudian – excrement as a child's first works of art.

Eryl used Dr Benjamin Spock's *Baby and Child Care*, first published in 1946, as a reference book for child-rearing. It is matter-of-fact about constipation causing an anal fissure:

> Sometimes a child gradually or suddenly gets into a spell of unusually hard movements that are painful to pass … When a fissure has occurred, it is likely to be stretched open again each time another movement is passed. This is quite painful, and the fissure may thus be kept from healing for many weeks. You can easily see how a child who has once been hurt may dread a repetition and fight against toileting again. It may become a vicious circle, because if the child succeeds in holding back his movement for several days, it is more likely to be hard.

Constipation this bad was a source of shame to me.

Nowadays, any paediatrician seeing a child with an anal fissure would be on the look-out for signs of sexual abuse, which didn't happen to me. Is it an instance of early rebellion? I'm sure that shit and art are connected. To this day, I feel the approach of a good poem as a stirring in my bowels. It's an infallible sign that something genuine is happening. What exactly am I keeping for myself, at the age when I'm beginning to write diaries and poems? What is impossible to say out loud but is being expressed by my body refusing to 'perform'.

My parents know that helping me to poo is a job for Dad. Whenever I fail to defecate, or as he'd say, '*cael dy gorff lawr*' ('get your body down') for a couple of days, Dad sits on the side of the bath next to the toilet, keeping me company. No doubt such exclusive attention would, in itself, be an incentive to staying bound.

One bout of constipation stands out in my memory. Even Gwilym has failed to produce results one week. On a Saturday, he turns my bowel movement into a game. In whispers, he proposes that we give

Mam a big surprise and lets me know that, if I poo, I'll be rewarded with a sixpenny piece. So, I sit on the throne, straining. Dad has taught me to stroke my stomach from right to left with my hand, to help peristalsis. He squats, facing me and, in order to encourage me, holds up the sixpence between his thumb and forefinger, like a rising silver sun.

Success! I go downstairs to show Mam my coin and to receive praise for my efforts. Excrement pays – a good lesson for a future writer.

My mother is extremely careful of our teeth. When Eryl recalls breastfeeding me, she always brings up my biting her nipples, as if this were a deliberate act of aggression. Sweets are not allowed, except after lunch on Saturdays and Sundays as a treat. They're kept in the pink jar hidden in the sideboard. My sister and I are occasionally given some money to walk to Whitchurch village to buy Bazooka bubble gum, which is considered 'better for the teeth', as it's related to chewing gum. Disappointingly, the bubble gum always loses its flavour by the time we've walked home. Greedy, I can't help myself, and steal a tube of Toffos from the shop, the only time I ever did it. For once, I'm not found out.

The dinner ladies loom large in my life on the schoolyard, as they supervise us playing. They're English-speaking and I learn new words from them. Mrs Davies and Mrs Harries drink tea from sky-blue cups and saucers. It's considered a privilege to carry the china back with great care to the canteen. During break time, an older pupil is stationed at the school's doors, to prevent anybody from going in. Clutching the still-warm dishes, I find that I can enter the building if I use the formula:

'I've got permission.'

I have no idea what 'permission' means, but I know that it's an open sesame word, a spell that can open a door.

In infant school the milk break every morning is an ordeal. In the 1960s, the government supplies schoolchildren with a daily third of a pint, to help build teeth and bones. These drinks are delivered in crates to each classroom. When prompted by the teacher, we have to file past the crate and take a bottle and straw. Blue Tits have learned to peck a hole into the bottles' foil lids in order to sip cream that has risen to the top. You either puncture the foil top with your straw or remove it entirely with your thumb. The milk is always warm and makes me gag. Fortunately, some of the boys can be persuaded to drink my ration, as well as their own. When a few bottles are left in the crate and Miss Rees asks who hasn't had their milk, I never confess.

Mrs Davies, the dinner lady with the dyed black hair, specialises in helping children whose milk teeth are falling out and is good at persuading a loose incisor to stop clinging to its root. She's an excellent judge of tooth ripeness and is trusted to tie it to the door handle with thread and wait for someone to come through briskly, thus removing the tooth. She was also capable of executing the Pull Judicious. It's she who helps us to break the tooth's hymen, that final strand of meat attaching tooth to gum. The redundant bone can then be taken home as treasure.

In other ways, Eryl is generous with the sugar. She's started teaching again, so we're trusted to let ourselves into the house, have a snack and entertain ourselves until she comes home. She makes a chocolate cake that I still crave, though I haven't eaten it since I was ten. The sponge is dark with cocoa powder. On the top of the cake is a layer of melted milk chocolate so thick that it stands on its own after you've cut a slice and needs to be cracked open, like thick ice on a puddle. The filling is a generous wedge of butter cream, sometimes flavoured with coffee. If she hasn't had time to bake, she leaves us Wagon Wheels, massive chocolate biscuits that feel as big as our heads. Or there are Snowflakes, domes of a coconut-coated shell the same shape as a breast, containing whipped nougat. Walnut Whip is reserved for a Saturday or Sunday afternoon after toasted teacakes. It's shaped like a chocolate volcano, topped with a walnut, with a secret companion sunken in the cone's base. For these, we have permission.

What's Not Allowed is sweets on my own initiative. For junior school, our class has joined Ysgol Bryntaf, the first Welsh-language primary school established in Cardiff. This means that my sister and I can walk to and from Viriamu Jones, a Victorian building in Gabalfa. In order to reach the school, my sister and I have to go through the Mynachdy council estate. The residents don't seem to like us and gob on us as we pass. We share the site with another English-speaking school and relations can be hostile.

One day, on our way home from junior school, a sweet van is parked at the end of Mynachdy Road. I have enough money in my purse so, on impulse, I buy a chocolate bar. The moment I've done it, I know I'm in trouble. I try to persuade my sister to have some of the sweet, to silence her with her own complicity. She's too clever to fall for that. I have no memory of eating or enjoying the sweet because I'm now sick with anxiety about what I've done. Preparing myself for my doom, I compose a self-justifying note (full of a 10-year-old's spelling errors) to Eryl, trying to head off the row:

> *Annwyl Mam*
>
> *Ar y ffordd garter fe welais van ac yr oeth yn gwerthu loshin. Feddylies i faint o'n i yn caru Marian a dyma fi yn prynu* Mars Bar*[.] Rydych chwi yn meddwl siwt y gês i'r arian i'w bryni. Yn ysgol roedd Mr. Jenkins ddim gyda llawer o gnau. So dyma fe yn dweud 'rhanwch Gnau gyda Marian['] a dyma fe'n rhoi newid i fi. Rwy wedi ei fwyta yn lle y peth arall. Ac rwy wedd [sic] Bwyta afal a glynhai fy'n nanedd.*
>
> *Gwyneth*
>
> *xxxxx*

> (Dear Mam,
>
> On the way howm I saw van and itt was selling sweets. I thought how much I love Marian and I bought a Mars Bar[.] You are thinking how I got the money to buy itt. In school Mr. Jenkins didn't have many nuts. So he said 'Share with Marian['] and he gave me the change. I have eaten it instead of the other thing. And I haff eaten an apple and cleaned mine teeth.)

My claim that I bought the Mars bar out of love for my sister is a transparent lie. I wanted it for myself. I was mocked for years for it. I suspect that 'the other thing' I was meant to eat was a form of confectionery Eryl had left out for consumption after school.

When I'm clearing the best china cupboard after Eryl's death, I come across all my baby teeth in a classic Wedgwood pill box. The white cameo on a powder-blue jar shows the moment when the hero Paris chooses Aphrodite over Hera and Athena, giving her the Golden Apple. This was the beauty pageant that led to the Trojan War. If ever there was an example of making the wrong mythical choice, this is it. Opening the lid, I find seven teeth. Six are molars, three with fillings and four showing spots of decay. One crumbles in my fingers. The undersides resemble the black dots that run through a banana's centre, and are stained with what must be clotted blood. Before I'd seen the actual teeth, I'd felt sentimental that Eryl had kept a relic of my infancy, imagining that they were nestled there in innocence, like a bowl of snowdrops. What I have is a posh pot full of decay. These infant teeth are, literally, the ones that grow loose in nightmares and which I have to spit out like melon seeds, that archetypal drama of powerlessness and anxiety.

I'm already learning, as the Mars bar note shows, to try, as best I can, to head off occasions for conflict with Eryl. My father reproaches me with never anticipating what will upset her, as if the rules were obvious. He and my sister also suffer but they're more cunning than I am and, therefore, less often in the spotlight. I could never perceive these Thou Shalt Nots before I'd crossed the line and drawn down the divine wrath.

When I'm about seven, my class sends a folk-dancing group to the Urdd Eisteddfod in Llanrwst, up north in the Conwy valley. The Eisteddfod moves around Wales, and the host area offers visiting competitors accommodation with local people. I hit the jackpot and am billeted in a farmhouse at the top of the mountain, which is my idea of heaven. Rather than condemning us to wearing the usual scratchy Welsh woollen skirt, apron and shawl in warm Whitsun weather, we dance in beautiful A-line contemporary dresses in turquoise, pink and lime-green psychedelic swirls, complete with a bow at the neck. We really fancy ourselves and are excited about updating tradition with contemporary fashion. We dance in one of the prelims, expecting to be praised for originality and flair. The judges hate it and we're not even placed.

When we gather on the coach that is taking us home, I notice that I've left the Tupperware which contained my sandwiches up at the farmhouse. Mr Jenkins, my teacher, tells me, reasonably enough, that he's sure that my mother won't miss one plastic container. He doesn't understand that I'm petrified, so I up the ante:

'*Ond hwnna yw* Tupperware *gore Mam.*'

('But that's Mam's best Tupperware.')

I know that this is ridiculous and that I'm putting the man to an amount of trouble entirely out of proportion with the value of a plastic container, but my terror of Eryl won't let me off the hook. There must be an urgency to my appeal because Mr Jenkins caves and, while the coach waits, he drives all the way up the mountainside to retrieve the container. He doesn't know that he's saving me from damnation. The incident becomes a family joke but what it tells me every time I hear it is how afraid I am of my mother.

Later on, Mr Jenkins has his own taste of Eryl's ferocity. When I fail to grasp long division, he hits me over the back of my hand with a ruler. Eryl goes up to the school to see him. It doesn't happen again. If she was on your side, Eryl could be a powerful ally.

Permission becomes a flash point between my mother and me. It's one thing to need the word as a passport to take crockery into school at break-time, but quite another to work out what I'm permitted to do on my own initiative. Eryl has terrified me out of trusting my own judgement. In childhood, that confidence isn't a renewable resource: once it's shouted out of you, it's gone.

There are the rows for doing nothing wrong at all. When I'm in Miss James's class in junior school, I begin to take violin lessons. The peripatetic music teacher visits the school on a Friday and, when it's your turn, you leave your classroom to scrape out

Twinkle, twinkle, little star on a three-quarter-sized fiddle, which the county education authority has lent you. When I reach home, Eryl asks me if I had Miss James's permission to leave her classroom. When she finds out that I hadn't – I didn't think I needed to – she wipes the floor with me. Eryl is a teacher herself and this adds to her righteous anger at my arrogance and defiance. The whole weekend is miserable. I walk to school especially early on the Monday morning, in order to see Miss James before class. I've been instructed to apologise for being so disobedient. By the time I have a chance to speak to Miss James, I'm in floods of tears, believing that I've committed a terrible act of disrespect. Miss James is astonished and tells me that I've done nothing wrong and ends up comforting me for being so upset. She can't restore the awful weekend of being frozen out that I'd just endured. Miss James's reaction showed that I've made a correct assessment of what good behaviour consists of in her class. This remains secret knowledge, there's no place for it at home.

Over the years, as a family, we develop an eccentric pattern of eating. Because both parents work and we girls are busy with after-school activities, during the week we never eat together. When we have time, we each take the makings of a salad from the fridge and eat to our own schedule. My father never has lunch, but a cup of coffee and a slice of home-made fruitcake with cheese. In the evening he, too, makes himself a salad. The only meal we gather around the table for is Sunday lunch, which, in years to come, becomes an instrument of torture for me.

Eryl is a baking virtuoso. She speaks her love in sugar. When my parents are elderly, Leighton and I visit regularly for a chat. It's not unusual for Eryl to open colourful well-worn tins and offer us three kinds of home-made biscuits. We usually leave with a batch of warm cookies in a greaseproof-lined tin. She makes a supply of fruit cakes for Dad, ranging from *bara brith* (a traditional Welsh fruit bread), to boiled fruit cake (called Vera's cake, as Eryl had the recipe from the school cleaner). Richest of all was Dundee cake. The latter is so full of fruit and nuts that it's expensive to make and is reserved for special occasions. She decorates the top with alternating green and red glacé cherries. It counts as a birthday present or a Christmas gift. I joke that it has so much fruit in it that it's practically salad.

Sugar, therefore, is provided for us as adults, but not more urgent fare. One Christmas, Leighton and I are due to fly from Heathrow to Andalucía for the holidays. Unbeknownst to us, Leighton is suffering from non-Hodgkin lymphoma and, so, his immune system is compromised and he succumbs to food poisoning. In the airport hotel we stay in the night before flying, he begins vomiting violently and exploding with diarrhoea. It's clear the following morning that we can't go, so we visit a local doctor for a medical certificate in order to claim on our travel insurance. Neither of us has slept much and, by the time I drive us home to Cardiff, I can't face the crowds in the supermarket.

I have no food in the house so, in desperation, phone Mam to ask if she can feed us. She refuses, giving no reason.

I'm stunned. The phrase that comes to me – Sunday school attendance has meant that I know my Bible – is Christ asking his disciples: 'Is there anyone among you who, if your child asks for bread, will give a stone?' (Matthew 7:9) We don't even get a stone.

After Eryl dies, I find myself eating compulsively. If I'm driving anywhere, I stop at shops and buy carrier bags full of confectionery and crisps, which I scoff in the car and dispose of the evidence. Shrinkflation means that the packages are much smaller than I remember, so I buy double the number. Sometimes I try to confine myself to a couple of squares of posh dark chocolate, but end up scoffing the whole bar. I never feel full; my satiety indicator is broken. I gulp down bars of chocolate-covered caramel, Mars bars, Mint Aeros and push barely chewed Haribos – especially the sweets covered in bitter sugar – down my own gullet. I eat peanut butter with a spoon from the jar. I stop keeping it in the house but turn to tahini, which is also sweet. The more I eat, the more pressing grows my hunger. I crave the sensation of being gorged, to feel my insides – throat, gullet, oesophagus and stomach – swell with warmth. What I'm wanting is the sense of being alive and safe in my own body.

Soon I no longer want to eat in public, because it's not usual to have three servings of ice-cream sundaes with all the trimmings while your colleagues are watching. If there's food available on an occasion, I can't forget about it until it's all finished and hoover other people's plates. At a conference, I can't leave the sponge squares alone at teatime and hate myself for returning repeatedly to pile up my plate. When I'm teaching away, I eat a full dinner and then secret supplies of pretzels and crisps, cheese and crackers.

One day, I'm waiting behind a woman in a pharmacy. She's leaning her elbow on the counter and, in the same hand, has an unwrapped chocolate in her fingers, tantalisingly close to my face. I can smell it. I wish that she'd eat her sweet, out of the way, but she's engaged in an endless conversation with the pharmacist. It's inconceivable to me that a person could hold a chocolate without eating it immediately. I have to struggle with myself not to grab it from her hand with my teeth and gobble it down, like a dog. It would serve her right.

I ask a psychiatrist friend about this development and he speculates that, for a baby, eating as many calories as possible would be an adaptive strategy for survival, if the mother is in danger. Logically, it makes some sense that my monstrous greed was partly a grief reaction. Even though I'm a grown woman, my reptilian brain has registered that I'm now motherless and is instructing me to stock up. I'm replacing the sugary maternal breast milk – later provided by Eryl in the form of biscuits and cakes – with my own carbs and sweets.

The most stubborn part of this rapidly developing addiction is night eating. I wake and my defences are down so, like a ghost, make my way down to the kitchen to make myself toast. I also binge on cereals, even dry Shredded Wheat, not generally known as an addictive substance. When I'm out of crackers, even the dog's kibble looks tempting. Before going to bed I barricade the kitchen door with chairs, feeling sure that this will remind me of my resolution not to binge but, like a giant, I scatter the ramparts built against my appetite. This is the night feed from which I can't wean myself, leaving me feeling guilty in the morning for my inability to discipline myself.

Now that the possibility of Mam feeding me had disappeared, against my will my body is craving the high-calorie food that doesn't nourish but does comfort. I gain thirty-five pounds: I'm a plump baby again. What I'm really craving isn't food, but maternal trust and affection. My body knows that all possibility of receiving that has now gone for ever.

Chapter 4
WITNESSES

Aged seven, I find the thread that's going to lead me through life. It's intensely private but will lead me out of isolation.

I catch a glimpse of myself in an observation Eryl makes of me as a young child. We've been visiting friends in Swansea and I'm paddling in Caswell Bay, staring intently at the foam around my calves. Auntie Val and Eryl catch me in a moment of wonder, looking at the patterns of bubbles, the pulses of wavelets.

'What *is* she thinking about?' asks Auntie Val.

I know exactly what I was doing in this moment of rumination – inside, I'm reaching to translate that feeling into a sound perhaps, eventually, into words.

Out of the blue, I write my first poem. It lands, fully formed on the page. Not a little ditty but a whole epic about the rain. I'm seven years old (same age as the start of the diary) and I begin writing spontaneously in order to entertain myself during a wet Easter holiday. I turn the tables on the rain by making it a subject, rather than an obstacle to pleasure. It's hardly a distinguished piece of work, but its neat four-line stanzas march down the pages in ways that satisfy me more than anything else I'd done before. Miss Rees, my primary school teacher, told me recently that I was the only pupil of hers ever to come to school knowing how to start and finish a story. Prose is all very well but this 'story' glitters with rhyme and

I find the struggle to fit sense into a pattern deeply absorbing. My protagonist is a boy called Deio. Interestingly, this was my father's way of softening the way of saying 'Damn!', so my hero is a disguised expletive. Rebellion is growing. The poem's story lurches around:

O mae'n bwrw glaw	Oh, it's raining,
Mae dŵr ar fy llaw	There's water on my hand
Mae awr yn mynd	An hour has gone
O dyma fy ffrind.	Oh here's my friend.
… *Dyma gawod arall eto*	… Here's another shower
Rheda mewn i'r tŷ, Deio	Run into the house, Deio
O dyna dro gwael	Oh that's bad luck
Fi yw'r ail.	I am second.
…	
Glaw a baw, Glaw a baw	Rain and muck, Rain and muck
O Deio taw	Oh Deio be quiet
Mae'r ieir yn y clos	The hens are in the yard
Mewn awr bydd yn nos.	In an hour it will be dark.[5]

Writing is a way of dressing up in words, of putting on a verbal persona, like a costume. It's a performance that enables me to enter into a wider mind than my own, the secret life of language. I've found my medium.

I'm hugely proud of my achievement and show it to Eryl. She's extremely pleased with me and joins in the fun. Her way of doing that is to make changes to my poem in a teacher's red ink. She 'marks' it, correcting its inventive spelling, smoothing out the grammar, leaving a network of red lines over the oblong stanzas which have given me so much pleasure. At the time, I take this detailed attention as praise and bask in the attention. But I also

5 I've given another account of this incident in my *Sunbathing in the Rain: A Cheerful Book about Depression (London: Fourth Estate, 2006), pp. 33–5..*

resent the intrusion of red ink over my pencilled stanzas and their cocky parade down the pages. A spider has set an indelible web over my structures, of which I was so proud.

Now, I know so much more about how the poet needs to protect their work from others' interference that I'm horrified. Here was a joyful romp in verse, an instinctive splurge of rhythm, and it's been subjected to the criteria used for essays and schoolwork, a fundamental misunderstanding of the source of writing's dynamic. It hurts. Alice Miller calls this behaviour by a mother 'poisonous pedagogy' because it's an attempt to control and direct the child's inner world.[6] Ever the teacher, Eryl is laying the groundwork for 'better' poems in the future. Whenever I teach poetry to young children in schools, I first have to counter the improving influence of the teacher and encourage the pupils not to worry about writing 'proper' Welsh. Once the children understand that their way of talking is what I'm after, they begin to write with colloquial flair, and we're away.

What I needed, more than correction, was a sixpenny piece of unqualified admiration.

Eryl notes my interest in words and, in the next few years, does everything she can to encourage it. In *Y Cymro* ('The Welshman'), the weekly Welsh-language newspaper, a person called Dewythr Tom ('Your Uncle Tom') runs a weekly poetry competition for children. At the end of the column, which consists of the previous week's winning poems, the subject for the following week is announced. There are postal orders to be won.

We settle into a pattern of producing work. I make some kind of draft and then we edit together. I'm eager to learn from Eryl. The poems are always based on what I write but are so heavily re-worked that they become something else. As you'd expect of an English teacher, Eryl has a real feel for poetry and teaches me to expand what I can do with words. I'm hooked. She shows me how

---

6 Quoted in Terri Apter, *Difficult Mothers: Understanding and Overcoming Their Power* (New York: W.W. Norton, 2012), p. 82.

to approach a competition's set subject from an unexpected angle, how to create a logical story with emotional crescendos formed by grouping words that sound the same together. She teaches me to use alliteration and, also, to use the Welsh-English *Geiriadur Mawr* ('The Big Dictionary') to give me a wider choice of vocabulary.

I'm sure that she's not the only parent helping her child along in this way; it would have been expected in Welsh-speaking circles. But I'm uneasy. I know that this isn't, strictly speaking, my work.

One week, the subject is '*Dawns y Lliwiau*' ('The Dance of Colours'). I recently found this on a typewritten sheet (I couldn't type at that age, so Eryl must have done it). We choose to imagine how each shade would dance if they were at a ball:

Suai'r Gwyrdd yn foesgar
I'r Porffor rhadlon teg,
Disgleiriai'r Aur yn eirias.

(Green was humming graciously
To Purple, beautiful and serene,
Gold sparkled, white-hot.)

The Red is imagined as a conqueror, intent on taking over the dance, in what becomes a drama of domination. This story of a colour growing in confidence and taking over echoes the unfolding drama between Eryl and me:

Cadfridog coch yn goresgyn,
Yn chwyrnelli'n farus,
Yn llyncu gwawr y Gwyrdd,
Y Glas gwangalon.

(A red Colonel conquers,
Whirling greedily,
Swallowing Green's hue,
The weak-hearted Blue.)

As I translate these lines for you, I can feel that the work is good. There are no extraneous words; something happens, and there's a euphony of consonants adding to the drama. But would I have known the word '*cadfridog*' ('colonel') at eight years old? '*Milwr*' ('soldier'), yes, but I smell Eryl's 'strengthening' of my draft with alliterative vocabulary. From week to week we win and eagerly await the subject for the following competition.

What Eryl and I are producing are collaborative texts. I'm engaged in Writing with Mother. I bask in her approval. While we're editing together, there's peace in the house and, therefore, redemption for me. With my mother – compass of my bliss and misery – I'm invincible. I'm doing what I love best with a keen companion who can help me improve. I like winning and it keeps me safe from maternal strife. To this day, I long for such a figure but have never found an artistic partner like Eryl. Part of me basks in Mam's special attention. Another part resents her pushing and feels uneasy about how much she's helping me.

I owe the kind of writer that I am now to Eryl. Perhaps I'm being ungrateful.

—*This was where it started, a parasite using her host.*
—*I'm sorry, I should have refused her help.*
—*How could you have at that age? Eryl was feeding on you.*
—*She was nourishing her child.*
—*No child should be a ventriloquist's doll.*

I'm paralysed between two perspectives, my own and Eryl's. At about the same age, I have an accident that feels like the physical equivalent of the situation in which I find myself. I'm playing on a metal swing outside, balancing along the horizonal bar of the A. Suddenly, I slip and my legs go either side. I scream because I'm split in two. The black, rusty metal leaves long grazes along the inside tendon of my right thigh, a muscle that tenses at the least provocation even now. Back as a sobbing child, I'm carried inside and comforted, but the remedy for the scrapes caused by my own weight falling is to sit, twice a day, in a shallow bath of salt water. It's the best remedy but God it burns.

A person, especially a child, should give prime importance to her own point of view while doing her best to imagine and take into consideration other people's. At the age I fell, I've already been cheated out of being my own authority. Eryl is forcing me to give primacy to her view of me, making my own assessment of situations secondary. She does this by emotional force. This has left me with a kind of insanity, in which I'm unable to know what I really think about something, especially if it clashes with my parents' views, because the prospect of any conflict is too frightening. From this accident onwards, I also think of my two languages as footholds on either side of a fissure. Unless I balance extremely carefully, switching languages and cultures risks tearing me apart.

And yet, and yet … One week the competition subject is a doll. The toy I imagine is haughty, looks at me with contempt:

Y Ddol	**The Doll**
Dyna lle 'roedd hi –	There she was,
Yn eiste'n orseddfawr	Sitting, enthroned
Ar gadair sigledig,	On a rickety stool,
Ag ystum ffug ar ei hwyneb.	A fake smirk on her face.
Syllais arni.	I stared at her.
Ei ffrog goch yn danbaid,	Her red dress fiery, strong,
a chryf	
Ei gwallt aur mewn	Her golden hair in fancy ribbons,
rhubanau ffansi,	
Bochau coch, mileinig –	Red cheeks, malicious –
Brenhines y doliau,	Queen of the dolls,
Yn greulon,	Cruel,
Yn gyfrwys.	Cunning.
Teflais hi i'r gornel.	I threw her to the corner.

I'm no longer sure who wrote this poem, but I know that the dramatic flourish in the final line is mine. It's difficult to know who the doll is a proxy for, me or Eryl. Perhaps it describes, from both sides of the mirror, our mutual hostility. Mothers and daughters are meant to love each other, so those who don't have to speak in code.

—I tried to be Mother's Good Doll.
—Daughter Doll is supposed to disobey. It's her sacred duty.

'Gwyneth stood up with help of sewing machine', notes Eryl in her house log for 5 June 1960. This instrument was central to life in the Lewis home. The cover for this model of Singer is elegantly rounded, with the curved tin-sheeting shape of a rural Welsh barn. Inside the casing is an elegant black appliance with gold filigree patterns traced on it and, in Gothic letters: 'The Singer Manufacturing Co.' On the side of the contraption is the fold-out handle that drives the rise and fall of the needle. I turn it tentatively and hear Mam at work again. The mechanism has weight and runs smoothly, a sign of good engineering. This utensil was the muse of my early years: 'Sing!' it said, 'Together, we sing, dance, perform!' For many years, Eryl used the Singer from her mother's house. It's the only object, aside from the Crugeryr clock, that I wanted to keep from my childhood. Both are linked by their time-keeping properties. When my mother was sewing at full speed and confidence, this sound had the hypnotic effect of a railway carriage's metal rhythm, comforting, the sign of progress being made and God being in his heaven.

Eryl could always be counted on to produce costumes of quality and panache. First year in primary school, aged five, our class dresses up to present a play for the parents. The two main characters are the Babes in the Wood. I'm to play Twti Glyn Hec, the witch. The girls are daffodils, their faces framed by flowers made from yellow crêpe paper, while the boys are kitted out as trees, in brown tights with green crêpe-paper branches. I wanted to be a tree. My part requires dress-making. Eryl cuts an old black watered-silk evening skirt of hers into a cloak and, giving it a smart standing collar, attaches the ends to my wrists with elastic. There's so much material that I can throw deliciously evil flourishes. She also makes a tall conical hat out of cardboard painted black with glued-on foil crescent moons and stars. The finishing touch is a set of plastic hag nails that slide over the tips of my fingers. We do things thoroughly in our house so we paint them with red varnish.

Miss Rees, my teacher, adds make-up, covering my face in black powder paint. I have the utmost confidence in my costume and made my entrance with gusto:

Ha ha ha,	Ha ha ha,
Hi hi hi	Hi hi hi
Twti Glyn Hec	Twti Glyn Hec
Yw fy enw i!	Is my name!

I remember nothing about the dialogue but, after Twti has attempted to do mischief to the children and been defeated, I've been instructed to give a loud scream and cackle as I leave the stage. I give it my all. Nobody tells me that the audience would laugh in appreciation of such a wholeheartedness. I rush to the girls' toilet, sobbing, tears leaving grey streaks down my face. Miss Rees tries to explain that the parents were laughing because they liked me, but I'm inconsolable. Nobody can persuade me that this isn't disgrace.

Years later, I meet Miss Rees again and we reminisce about the incident. She recalls thinking at this time:

'This girl has no idea what success is.'

Nor do I now.

I open a dusty trunk and gasp. I'm clearing my parents' house and discover unexpected presences. This tomb contains miniature beds, with matching pillows and sheets, a wardrobe of fashion outfits and accessories, games for the amusement of dead royalty: all the funerary goods tiny beings would want on their journey to the otherworld. In another case, I find the implacable faces of our childhood dolls. These are the gods of my girlhood. They've been here, waiting for me, the apostate, all these years. In keeping these idols, Eryl has been the high priestess of this domestic cult, leaving us the old gods to reckon with long after her own death.

Suddenly I catch the glint of kinder eyes. As my heartbeat slows, a simian face composes itself from the shadows. The skin is a velvet that my lips know well. It belongs to a glove puppet I've completely forgotten about but whom I recognise as a familiar. He has auburn fur, the touch of which turns me back into a child. Pushing my giant adult hand into the puppet, I bring my ear to his mouth and we immediately resume our conversation from my pagan childhood.

—*You took your time.*
—*Mwnci, it's you! So it's your voice I've been hearing.*
—*I wasn't far away, in a part of your brain.*
—*My witness.*
—*I saw everything and never forget. And I'm on your side.*
—*Not always a comfortable place to be.*
—*Where else are you ever going to stand? I'm a secret friend.*
—*I've been confused for so long.*
—*Together, we'll work it out, this disentangling.*

I'm seven or eight when Mamgu dies, leaving Eryl with a slipped disc after the heavy lifting of nursing her. She spends six weeks in traction at Rhydlafar Hospital in Cardiff. Contrary to current practice, which is to encourage movement, Eryl is confined to bed, the mattress angled at forty-five degrees and feet above her head. A heavy black counterweight at the bottom of the bed frightens me, with its suggestion of violence and stopped time. I feel desperately sorry for my mother's pain. It's hard to reach Eryl for a satisfactory cuddle.

Throughout our childhood, we have more dolls and their accoutrements than we need. Eryl dresses them smartly. A doll's quality was, as far as I was concerned, dependent on her underwear. Whenever I'm handed a doll, I tip her upside-down and inspect her support garments. My Siwan Elen, for example, wears aquamarine layers, to 'keep her kidneys warm': a woollen skirt, woollen trousers underneath, both covered by a stout cardigan and topped with a hat which has a long taper and ending in a pom-pom. I have the same hat, scaled up to a larger size in red for winter.

Eryl's sewing skills extend to making toys, as well as their clothes. One Christmas, my sister and I are presented with identical rag dolls. Raggedy-Ann and Jemimah Jane were big – about half my height and even larger in comparison with my sister. They have thick brown woollen plaits, most satisfactory, and moss-green dresses pleasingly decorated with red rick-rack. These dolls' expressions are made of felt pieces stuck onto the cloth. It doesn't take me long

Showing off Raggedy-Ann and Jemimah Jane and Christmas dolls, 1964 (Gwyneth has mumps and chicken pox)

to pull the side of my Raggedy-Ann's smile loose, leaving a smear of dark-coloured glue at the mouth. Each doll has a home-made wicker rocking cradle. Eryl also makes footstools, baskets and, memorably, a set of Indonesian shadow puppets.

While she's in hospital, Eryl passes the long days knitting a wardrobe for our dolls. By that time, we've moved on from Sindy, Tressy (Barbie's never allowed, too vulgar) to Teeny Tiny Tears, a baby doll that would 'drink' from her bottle and appear to shed real tears and, best of all, to wet her nappy. Clearing the loft, when I find a certain dress knitted in neon pink nylon with holes for a ribbon to gather under the bust, I feel sick with anxiety. Holding this forgotten dress in my hands, I can feel Eryl's unhappiness as plainly as if it were my own.

Tiny dolls like Pee Wee, Itsy Bitsy and Liddle Kiddles have become fashionable, including the hugely popular Trolls that have wizened faces and long tufts of fluffy red hair. Not one of them is taller than three inches and yet Eryl knitted and sewed full sets of clothes for them. My favourite costume is a knitted black flamenco dress, with a drop waist and a full skirt of loops in flounces. The handwork is tiny and beautiful, but I can't forget the pain that's behind this displacement activity. It must have been agony for Eryl to work, lying in traction, with her hands higher than her head. For this reason, I was never able to play with those clothes without a twinge of conscience, as if I'd caused the trial by traction myself. I didn't, of course, but by now, I can't distinguish between things that are my fault and those that are not.

I think that during our early years as children, Eryl was bored. Gwilym was in work all day and a creature of staid habit when at home. She knits her frustrations into the clothes she made for our dolls but also into our brains. Every mother crafts her own child's body and her interaction with her offspring shapes the neural grid of that child's future emotional capabilities. She crochets an internal filigree, like a christening shawl, that sets the dominant pattern for life.

Eryl was an expert and talented seamstress, who could run up a dress in a day and, even, work without a pattern. She once made a pink tutu to a professional standard, a feat that still amazes me. She was brought up in the generation that learned how to sew, knit and practise other handcrafts as a matter of necessity. In the 1960s, when my sister and I were raised, shop clothes were expensive and offered a limited variety of styles, so Eryl sewed many of our outfits until we left home.

Because she was a perfectionist, the clothes Eryl made us were stylish and functional. An early dress she sewed that I remember was made from a Simplicity Pattern 4878 for a girl aged six. The cover of the envelope showed three confident girls holding lollipops. Oddly, the children stand with legs apart, in the so-called 'power pose' that Tory politicians adopted a few years ago; it was ridiculed so much that the stance was soon dropped. Eryl made my outfit in red, one of my favourite colours. Using ruffled layers of white broderie anglaise, she sewed an appliqué daisy, which I enjoyed, to the skirt. To this day, my body's never more comfortable than in a well-made dress of high-quality cotton, with pockets.

When my sister came along, Eryl would make matching clothes for us in two sizes. One such was Simplicity 3846, a sundress with tie straps and smocking stitched to the yoke. Eryl chose contrasting gingham – pink for me, yellow for my sister – and improvised matching boleros with ruched white lace sewn into the neck seam. She was, rightly, so proud of these outfits that she kept them as souvenirs in a trunk. They're so beautifully sewn that I can't bring myself to throw them.

On another trip to Ceredigion, Marian and I wear matching dresses made of a fabric dotted with rosebuds, a shocking pink tie and home-made cardigans in light blue. I'm in the power pose and already growing too tall for my dress.

The dressmaking process was very stressful for all concerned. There is a shortness of temper which is more pervasive than the understandable tension of being engaged in tricky work. Eryl could

Marian and Gwyneth in dresses made by Eryl

be petulant, mixed with a peevish shade of fury. When I think of Eryl, she was very often '*crac*' with me. '*Crac*' is a wonderful Welsh word, not to be confused with the Irish craic. Derived from 'crack or fissure' it's 'a loud, sharp noise', and it means 'hot-headed, irascible, rash, angry, mad'.[7] The process of having these beautiful

7 *Geiriadur Prifysgol Cymru* (University of Wales Dictionary).

clothes sewn was so worrying that it left me feeling guilty that making my clothes was leaving Eryl so miserable.

In early years, we wear what we are given but, as we grow, Eryl consults us on our preferences. We start out in hope, searching through huge Butterick and Simplicity pattern books in the shop, half bored, half mesmerised. This requires long, indecisive visits to David Morgan's or Howells', Cardiff's biggest department stores. Choosing the material is even more of an ordeal.

'*Ti'n lico hwn? Beth am hwn?*'

('Do you like this? What about this?')

There's much agonising about the thickness of material and whether there's enough of it to match the pattern across seams. Once Eryl has chosen, the shop assistant measures out the cloth in yards, using a long brass ruler fixed to the side of a big table. The length has to be generous enough to fit us while, at the same time, not being wasteful. The atmosphere is tense, and I always watch the assistant running her scissors along the fabric at the final measurement with trepidation. The scissors eat the fabric with a hugely satisfying rasp and scrunch.

Any mention of cutting out the pattern at home strikes fear into my heart. Eryl pins the tissue paper pattern on the material, thinking hard about optimal use of the fabric. If you dare to approach her during the process of cutting, you're shouted at and, if you're wise, flee. Then comes the equally painful process of fitting. Eryl pins the pieces of cut material together. Gingerly, I thrust in an arm, trying not to be stabbed by the pins or to tear the loosely tacked pieces apart. If I move over-enthusiastically, the seam comes undone, and there's shouting and slapping of arms, or whichever part of the body that caused the pattern to part. I'm always fascinated to watch red finger marks fade on a calf or upper arm.

It's a huge relief when I'm made to stand on a chair and hear the chalk puffer marking out the line of a hem. I turn in a slow circle in my finery, like a ballerina in a music box.

When I'm in charge of my own costume, my approach is minimalist. Eryl puts together a fancy-dress box and, one afternoon in July 1967, all the girls on the street come to our house to have a fancy-dress competition. Catholics Jillian and Madelaine bring their

First Communion wreaths and dresses. My best friend Elaine finds a bride's veil and makes herself a posy. Julie staggers around in oversized high-heels and a party dress belonging to her mother, the fearsome Mrs Cronin, who keeps a cane above the sitting-room mirror. My sister is wearing the Twti Glyn Hec witch outfit. I adopt a radical strategy. I take two chiffon scarves, roll one up as a bra, fix the other as a veil and push an old petticoat down to my hips. You can see my baggy knickers through the petticoat's nylon. I'm a belly dancer.

Fancy dress party, July 1967

It's surprising how many problems can be solved with the strategic deployment of two chiffon scarves and a slip.

I'm awake one night, about aged ten, but already I know that, more than anything, I want to think, read and write. In my mind, I'm making a promise to God and to myself. I want to be stretched by the way I live intellectually and creatively, to feel that give and growth achieved in partnership with … something that isn't me and which is joy, clarity and sound.

This is the single most important decision I will ever make in my life. Without knowing it, this is the only chance I have of surviving the personal catastrophe that's unfolding at home. This internal spiritual gesture means that the most important part of me is placed out of my own and other people's reach. This is an otherlife – not an afterlife – that has made everything possible for me.

I don't suppose it was unrelated to the approach of puberty. Writing's erotic for me; it requires a gentle but persistent search for pleasure through rhythm. I've found my clitoris, which gives access to a new fundamental force in my universe. At around the same time, a lime-green pamphlet appears on my bed, explaining about my ovaries, which look like the head of a Praying Mantis. Eryl enquires how I'm getting on with my sex education book and I inform her that I've reached the bit about Virginia. By the time I'm ready to make sense of it, the booklet has disappeared.

One of the curses – and blessings – of the Welsh-language poetry tradition is the dominance of the *eisteddfod*, which offers competition as a method of practising the arts. This happens at local, regional and national levels. The Urdd holds its own festival at Whitsun every year. In my last year at junior school, the set subject in the under-12 category is '*Adar*' ('Birds'). Eryl takes the initiative and, to my mind, crosses a line.

The opening – '*Rhyw gyffro cynnar yn y coed*' ('Some early excitement in the trees') – is effective but that's definitely Eryl's rhythm, not mine. It's an adult's imitation of a child's writing and, of course, wins first prize. Eryl's stolen my identity and I can't tell anyone. Winning seems to be a good thing, but I feel doubly dirty because I both enjoy the attention and felt deeply embarrassed by it. I feel like a cheat and I can't tell anyone.

Even then, I'm in the habit of keeping a notebook by the side of my bed and scribbling down tinder words that can spark into a poem. I don't need help to write naturally, so why was Eryl pushing me?

One day in class during the final year of junior school, we're set a task – to write a short prose piece imagining that we'd been present at the crucifixion. I write with complete unselfconsciousness and emotional abandon and know I've produced something powerful.

It's like riding a lion. My teacher marks it nine out of ten and praises my work aloud. I wish she hadn't. I don't want Eryl – or anybody else – to see it, so I tear the piece out of my exercise book and throw it in the bin. This exercise is entirely my own work but my relationship to it was already compromised by the fear of it being co-opted. I bet the writing was very, very good.

Any poet knows that it's a short step from destroying your own work to doing the same to yourself.

—*This is the energy your God gave you. It's your muse, and yours alone.*

—*Where did Eryl's muse go?*

—*Locked in its own cage.*

—*Poor Eryl.*

—*Don't waste your compassion, she's stolen your lion. You need to push the bitch off.*

And where was your father in all this? Preoccupied.

Gwilym's first post in Cardiff is in the Port Health Authority, which combines his training in sanitary inspection and his familiarity with ships from his time in the Royal Navy. He cycles from Whitchurch to the docks every day. Sometimes, I meet him at the top of our hill and am rewarded with a thrilling freewheel down on the bike's crossbar. On 10 February 1966, the *Western Mail* publishes a feature on Gwilym's work. The journalist visits the 'almost Dickensian office', which I remember from occasional visits as a child, when I clamber up an exciting rotating chair with a crimson cushion tied to its laths, in order to reach scribbling paper on the oak rolltop desk. Although the volume of traffic through Cardiff's docks has declined, Gwilym explains that 'London is the country's butcher shop, Liverpool its grocery, and Cardiff a sort of small general store'. In order to do his work, the inspector 'uses his nose, then his eyes and then will listen to or feel a tin':

> Mr. Lewis recalled a large load of tinned tomatoes which looked perfect but a random sampling test showed a high lead content and the whole consignment was condemned and destroyed.[8]

The largest part of Gwilym's work, therefore, was preventing toxins from harming human health.

He was less careful at home. We ate fire-damaged mint chocolates for a while, with a white bloom in the confection. Sometimes, we benefitted from 'fridge breakdown' food, which always had a question mark over it in my mind. In the 1980s, when it was revealed that many eggs produced by British hens were infected with salmonella, I phoned Dad for advice:

'It's all a big fuss. Do as you always do.'

His work gives us all a macabre interest in what's harmful to human health. One day, he comes home with the tale of a member of the public bringing in a tin of pears with a foreign object in it. On inspection, it turns out to be a severed human finger.

One evening, after he's picked me up from a ballet lesson, Gwilym takes me on a noise nuisance call. A man has complained about a hum. Gwilym has agreed to visit the area with a decibel meter, to measure sound levels at various times of day. We stand in the dark street of terraced houses, unable to hear anything. The needle on the dial doesn't move. I see Gwilym knock on the complainant's door and he answers, wearing a white shirt and black National Health Service glasses. Gwilym tells me that the man is being driven out of his mind by the noise, even though its existence can't be proved. Perhaps the hum is inside his head. I believe the man, even though the machine doesn't register the cause of his anguish. To this day, that industrial low-frequency noise is widely reported between Bristol and Swansea. I hear it often.[9]

---

8 Peta Riley, 'Every Cargo Gets a Check', *Western Mail*, 10 February 1966.

9 See Jordan Tannahill, 'Can you hear the Hum? The mystery noise that says a lot about modern life', *The Guardian*, 7 July 2021.

In the family, I'm being driven to distraction. Nobody else seems to hear the same things as I do. In this noisy home, Gwilym's the one holding the decibel meter. Even though Eryl's treatment of me roars like a storm through my body. I'm being told that I'm the problem. Couldn't I be more tactful? More practical? Mam is suffering more than any of us, so couldn't I just do as I'm told?

Gwilym completed his qualifications as a public health inspector three months before I was born. The final section of his exams dealt with smoke pollution. Eryl bought him a copy of *The Conan Doyle Stories* and wrote in the following dedication:

Gwilym Lewis *Gorffennaf 1959*	(Gwilym Lewis July 1959
Oddiwrth Eryl, *i ddathlu llwyddiant* *yn y* 'Smoke's Inspectors' *Diploma*	From Eryl to celebrate success in the 'Smoke Inspectors' Diploma)

Paradoxically, Gwilym was a pipe smoker. Not for him was the light, fragrant pipe tobacco advertised by men with firm jaws wearing cardigans (though he possessed both). His tobacco was Condor, which came in the pouch in black oblong strips, like compacted peat. It smelled glorious, like deep volcanic soils, or humus found at the roots of jungle trees.

As a child, when Gwilym was out, I'd approach his smoking apparatus and suck on the pipe, which gave only the most bitter aftertaste of tobacco ash. It was as close as I dared approach to experiencing what was clearly such a compelling pleasure for my father. As soon as I could, I became an enthusiastic smoker myself, though I gave up decades ago. At Christmas, he'd smoke cigars so, when we went abroad, my sister and I were charged with bringing back 'the blackest, cheapest, strongest' cigarillos we could find. One of my migraine auras is a smoke hallucination (also a sign of an oncoming fit in epileptics). After he'd died, I'd often catch a whiff of Condor, at its most fresh, aromatic and enticing. And then I'd get a headache.

One of the reasons for taking up smoking is the perceived nonchalance it gives the smoker. Rather than a sign of confidence, though, I now see it as a tell for anxiety. It's an act of self-soothing, the deliberate slowing down of breathing, perhaps a difficulty in finding what to say. Lighting and smoking a pipe is a ritual, a meditative practice that hides its fatal nature.

I must have had the smell of smoke on my clothes throughout my childhood. Gwilym could only start the car first by lighting his pipe. We'd all get in the car and wait. Match would be applied to tobacco, vigorous sucking set the tobacco in the bowl alight and, eventually, the desired amount of smoke would be obscuring our views of each other. Only then did Dad waggle the gear stick to check it was in neutral, pull out the choke and turn the ignition key – as if the pipe were an essential primer for the internal combustion engine. It was infuriating. Eventually, he'd release the handbrake and our mobile cloud, never going higher than third gear, was off. We'd arrive at Sunday school or ballet class, smelling of hellfire.

I think of him now as a man hiding behind a smokescreen. He was putting up a gauze curtain between himself and the world. The pipe smoke around Gwilym made a speech bubble, but I still don't know what he was saying.

—*You do.*
—*He was blotting us out.*

I'm ten and this is the day on which, in my mind, my headaches started.

In attempting the high jump on the school sports day, I slip on the grass before the bar and slide under it, on the back of my head. This concussion may or may not have set off a lifetime of migraines. After school, my brain experiences more than my mind can bear. I'm not equal to the world, it's invading me. I struggle to see through jazzing patterns and throw up the strawberry jelly I had for tea, the fruit like clots of blood.

I'm admitted to Cardiff Royal Infirmary for observation, and woken every hour, to check I'm alive and haven't slipped into a coma. Nurses cajole me into having a blood pressure cuff slipped over my upper arm.

Dawn reveals that I'm in a ward of monsters. The only bed they could find for me is in adult ophthalmology. The patients are very sweet to me but the eyepatches and enlarged eyeballs through bottle-top glasses frighten me. I'm told that my father is coming to fetch me this morning, so I set to watching the door. I'm Persephone squinting up into the light at the entrance to the underworld, wincing, and wondering why her parent is so slow to arrive … I'm offered breakfast, but I refuse the pomegranate that might keep me in the underworld a second longer than necessary.

Such faith do I have in Gwilym's coming to rescue me before he goes to work at eight, that there's no point in my moving my eyes from the exit, or I'll miss his arrival, which is the one thing I need to make me well. There's a clock above the ward door and its workings are attached by the occipital nerves to my headache.

Gwilym is a reliable and dependable giver of lifts to our various childhood activities, so it's unlike him to be late. Incredibly, the starting time at Dad's office comes and goes. This is unendurable. I endure. I'm distraught by the time he arrives in the afternoon. By which time, I'm worse off than when I was admitted to hospital, suffering from concussion and also beside myself with the lack of my father. The torment of that wait makes my left eye throb now with looking and not finding the one I wanted to see more than I wanted to be well.

—You needed your father to stand up for you at home and he never did.

—He was doing his best in difficult circumstances.

My father used to call me Daughter Number One and my sister Daughter Number Two. This was factually correct, but always carried an overtone that made me uneasy. It wasn't that I was his favourite (much though I would have wished to have been), the moniker made me feel like a function, especially as he grew older and more dependent on us. If I went to him with a dilemma about a friendship, his advice was, invariably: 'Always look after Number One'. There is a form of self-care that does that in a constructive way, in the sense of acknowledging that a person who's unwell can't help anyone else until they have an excess of internal resources. Fair enough. In the New Testament, Jesus urges his followers to 'love thy neighbour as thyself'. Not more, but certainly not less.

—I'll say it, even if you can't.

—If I was Daughter Number One looking after Number One, why did I feel like I was being destroyed?

—Because Gwilym was Looking After Number One. Himself.

I learned all I could possibly wish to know about literature from Eryl but, from Gwilym, the single-minded selfishness that a writer needs to create a new world with her at its centre. Perhaps I owe my father more artistically than I'd realised, in obeying, at last, that drive to hold on to what only I know, for all the resistances of those closest to me.

I'm finally doing what Dad advised: I'm looking after number one.

Chapter 5
TOP

For Christmas 1971, I receive an excellent gift: a bright red five-year diary in a box with a golden lid and black bottom. Every calendar day is a whole page, divided into five 'slots', so that, as I write each day's entry, I can compare it with the previous year's account. The 1972 handwriting is minuscule and orderly – it was my first year in high school. As the narrative runs down the page through the years to 1975, my marks on the page become larger, messier. From 1976, onwards, I keep an ordinary A5 page-a-day desk diary with copious stickers on the cover, still my favoured format.

I've only re-read these diaries once – in preparation for writing this book – and I won't do so again. They shock me not because I've forgotten any of the incidents described – I've remembered everything – but because of the remorseless rhythm of events and the implacable intensification of pressure on me as a teen. Given that I've done so much reading about the effects of emotional abuse on a person's health. I watch my growing self in these diaries with the full adult knowledge of the price I've paid for this upbringing. We – the earlier Gwyneth, completely isolated and yet posting bulletins to a future reader, and me, the grown-up, learning my full history from that child – now form an alliance. Who's rescuing whom, I don't know, but this dialogue between us is better than either of us screaming on our own.

In the autumn of 1971, when I turned eleven, I start at Ysgol Gyfun Rhydfelen (Rhydfelen Comprehensive School), one of the first Welsh-language high schools in Wales. I've been educated in Welsh since age three in nursery school. Everything the school does is informed by a commitment to preserving the Welsh language. If you're caught speaking English, you're in trouble. We all become expert at switching languages mid-sentence as a teacher approaches.

Halfway through my first year, we move from Whitchurch to a white house on top of a hill overlooking Cardiff. I spend hours looking out at the view. At night, the streetlights sparkle, the rosary beads of traffic glinting along the main roads. The Flatholm lighthouse flashes three times every ten seconds, according to official sources (but three every five seconds, as far as Leighton and I can see). If the wind is in the right direction, the City Hall clock can be heard chiming. A fog horn sounds in the Bristol Channel, like a cow lowing for her calf. Some mornings, the Ely River rises above itself like a ghost, tracing its own course in mist.

The move makes us hopeful as a family. The huge windows with light pouring in promise sunny times. We have apple trees in the garden and a bird bath! We've escaped from a neighbour whose son had a drumkit and we all need quiet in order to do schoolwork, says Eryl. I'm in my first year of high school and the amount of homework is building.

Looking back, however, I wonder if my parents over-extended themselves financially to afford the new detached house. Gwilym gives up smoking for a while in order to save money. Eryl has moved to a different school to teach and hates it. Over-stretched and unhappy at work, she's often irritable at home. During episodes of depression or burnout, she bitterly accuses him of pushing her to continue in work because his wage isn't enough to live on and they needed her earnings, which were higher than his. He counters that she did better in work than staying, ruminating, at home. If Eryl says, 'Go away, I'm irritable', you run, because her voice holds the threat of a match being struck over her gasoline temper.

My diary for May 1973 gives a vivid account of my parents installing new windows in my bedroom. 'Swotting' is our word for studying for a test or exam.

> *Mi swotes i trwy'r dydd ac 'rwy'n fed up. Ar hyn o bryd mae Mam a Dad yn brysur yn rhoi'r ffenestri i gyd yn ôl yn* bedroom *fi – mae storom mellt a tharannau yn ymladd yn erbyn ei hun y tu allan! Fe fu'n rhaid i ni ddal cotau lan yn erbyn y ffenestr ac mae popeth yn wlyb. 'Roedd e'n braidd o farce – ond tipyn o storom!*
>
> (I swotted all day and I'm fed up. At the moment, Mam and Dad are busy putting all the windows back in my bedroom – there's a thunder and lightning storm fighting against itself outside! We had to hold coats up against the window and everything is wet. It was a bit of a farce – but quite a storm!)
>
> (20 May 1973)

By then, the hurricane was well and truly in the house.

High-school education in Welsh is less than a decade old and, therefore, an experiment. The staff and parents of Rhydfelen are highly motivated to make the school a success; therefore there's a strong emphasis on academic performance but also producing young people who have a thorough knowledge of and deep participation in Welsh-language cultural life. I recognise the figure of the Asian Tiger Mother in America pushing her children to excel, partly because she's determined to make personal efforts to mitigate the disadvantages of being in a cultural minority. In Rhydfelen, we have Dragon parents and Dragon teachers, who are pushing pupils to achieve.

Discipline is strict, school-uniform inspections are held in the early years, to check that the boys are wearing the correct dark socks and the girls the prescribed navy-blue or black underpants. My diary notes that on 13 February 1973, Mr Vale holds a name-tag inspection and I'm booked for three infractions, including not having my name sewn inside my coat. The headmaster and deputy head wear black academic gowns and flap around like vampires. The cane is used, but not publicly, as it had been in junior school. Mr Jeffreys, history, is in the habit of making offending students (which often includes the whole class) stand on their chairs in the classroom. If you're singled out, in addition, for a further reprimand, you have to hold the metal wastepaper bin, while taking notes. This is regarded as something of a joke until it isn't. One day our class mutinies and we all sit down. The bully has lost his power over us.

There is real human warmth in the school, too. It's the kind of place where people will go the extra mile for you. Mrs Eileen Beasley gives me lessons in *cynghanedd* during the mid-morning break at the back of the biology lab, showing me how to compose strict meter verses so full of alliteration that they make Anglo-Saxon prosody look loose. In winter, Mrs Lily Richards, who teaches music, urges us girls to wear vests under our blouses (so uncool!). When we take our music exams during a heatwave, she brings us frozen lollipops. When Miss Ruth Evans, English, catches a boy swigging a can of coke in her class on a hot afternoon, instead of confiscating it, she passes it round so that everybody can have a mouthful. I remember her reproaching one of the boys fondly and naturally in two languages at once: 'Don't be so *twp*!' ('Don't be so thick!') There's a good mix of children from Cardiff and the south Wales valleys. One of the very best things about the school is that, every two years, we perform an oratorio. No auditions are held so, if you want to take part, you can, even if you're tone-deaf. By the time we leave, most of us know two great choral works off by heart. I can still sing the alto part of Mendelssohn's *Elijah* and Verdi's *Requiem* in Welsh.

Because Rhydfelen is located just south of Pontypridd, Cardiff pupils have to travel ten miles or more there and back by bus. This means that the journey takes up a significant part of our day. One of the highlights for me is that a group of us start to play cards, flirting during games of Whist and Trumps. My favourite is Cheat, requiring the ability to lie and keep a straight face. My friends don't expect it of me, because I'm a 'good girl' in class, but I find I can lie outrageously. (I'm not a liar when I'm not playing Cheat, in case you're worried.) I must have let slip about our game at home, though, because Eryl forbids me to take a pack of cards to school, even though we're not betting. Someone else brings in a deck from then on and we continue to play. I learn to keep my mouth shut at home.

School's emphasis on good academic results is nothing compared with Eryl's determination that I excel. Initially, this takes the form of her helping me with projects and revision. At that point, I'm still grateful for her support and count Eryl as an ally. Like Ben James, her father, she's an excellent teacher and shows me how to organise my work. She also pushes me when I'm reluctant to apply myself and insists on over-fulfilling homework. She never refuses help if I ask for it. But she pushes too hard.

I take to the daily discipline of writing a journal, so I can trace my teenage experiences, living with my parents, with great accuracy – first in the red five-year diary and then in individual volumes. Already I'm suffering badly from headaches, with frequent visits to the school nurse for painkillers. I have a headache every Monday and, often, migraines a couple of times during the week. Sometimes when I'm suffering from a particularly painful attack, I feel as though I'm wearing a red-hot helmet, Girl in the Iron Mask. Emotional abuse doesn't inflict direct physical violence at the time but it has tangible bodily consequences. Knowing what I know now about chronic migraine, this abnormal pattern needed medical attention, though effective treatment was decades away. Family therapy is what was needed.

—Or someone to take a stand.
—I tried my best.
—That wasn't your responsibility …

I may well have thought that my diary was being read, even if it wasn't, so I hide it. Writing about Eryl, my tone is a grovelling appreciation that disguises fear. For example, 21 January 1973 is an eventful day because my father, who sometimes has access to unusual foods because of his work, brings home something exotic for tea:

> *Mi adolyges i trwy'r dydd heddiw – 'rwy'n taerai [sic] na gymera i Lladin na Daearyddiaeth yn Nosbarth 4. Fe geson ni* 'Quails' *i ginio (*fridge breakdown*) a oedd yn costi £1.27. 'Roedden nhw fel [f]fowlyn bach bach ac mi ges i goes un. Aeth Marian i'r Ysgol Sul tra 'rown i'n 'swoto' … Yn y nôs, mi swotes i eto. Mae Mam yn* wonderful *– er bod pen tost gyda hi, mae'n fodlon fy helpu i drwy'r amser. Hi yw'r person gorau yn y byd (+ Dad a Marian).*
>
> (I revised all day today – I swear that I won't take Latin or Geography in Form 4. We had 'Quails' for lunch (fridge breakdown) that cost £1.27. They were like a small chicken and I had the leg of one. Marian went to Sunday School while I was 'swotting' … In the evening, I swotted again. Mam is wonderful – even though she has a headache, she's willing to help me all the time. She's the best person in the world (+ Dad and Marian).
>
> (21 January 1973)

On 21 February 1973, I lose my reading glasses but note: '*Mae Mam wedi bod yn resymol am y mater – mae'n gwneud i fi i garu hi mwy*' ('Mam has been reasonable about the matter – it makes me love her more'). Mam being reasonable is not the norm. Something is wrong when a child expresses love for a parent when she doesn't lose her temper over a genuine accident. Four days later, I have a bugs project to do for biology: '*'Roedd Mam yn helpu fi. Hi yw'r person mwyaf unselfish 'rwy'n nabod.* I wish I were like that' ('Mam was helping me. She's the most unselfish person I know. I wish I were like that').

At the same time, I'm concerned that my parents are 'supporting' me more than feels right. One history task is to draw a poster plan of Caerleon's Roman camp. The plan keeps my parents occupied for a while. What they produce is a fine technical drawing (Dad) complete with labelling (Mam), but I have nothing to do with it. The requirement is fulfilled and the teacher gives it a good mark and says nothing. I know that many parents help their children with homework, that isn't the problem. Those parents also allow their offspring to fall short and both parties learn that it's not a disaster. My work has already been hijacked. More seriously, I'm being taught that failing – at anything educational – is absolutely unacceptable to my parents. By now, I'm hopelessly entangled in Eryl's ambitions for me, completely unable to make a stand for what I want to be without being knocked over emotionally. If I'm not over-achieving, I'm not safe; the only escape from the pressure is to be ill. This pattern becomes deeply set in my body. It's not sensible, but it is the only way that I know how to survive at home. Be Tops or be Out of Action. Come to think of it, this was Eryl's work pattern, so I've mimicked it well.

Positive comments about Mam being so generous gradually disappear from my diary as I have no defence against her relentless intrusiveness. I try to eliminate occasions for Eryl to upbraid me. I can have no peace at home unless I'm overperforming in school. Good isn't good enough for me, I have to be Top. But standing out is the last thing any sane teenager wants. High grades suit the school's agenda perfectly, so staff have no reason to question the cost for a student like me.

There's a kind of abuse that causes a child to behave too well, rather than acting out. Only one teacher ever has the insight to see that I'm disturbed. Nobody pays attention to a child who's conforming to or exceeding expectations. It takes a wise eye to see such compulsive behaviour as a sign of trouble. Twrog Jones, geography, observes the insane amount of homework that I do, takes me to one side and tells me gently but firmly that there's no need to work so hard – surely unusual feedback to a pupil. I look at him blankly, not because I don't know what he means but because I do. I have no way, though, of telling him that I feel like a hostage with a gun at her back. However much she might want to call for help, she's struck dumb, with only her eyes trying to telegraph her panic.

I'm twelve and the strain is showing physically. I'm so skinny that Mrs Knight, the physical education teacher, asks me if I'm eating enough. I'm certainly not anorexic, as I have a healthy appetite, but I have no flesh on me. My body's changing. On 14 January 1972, after being in a choir rehearsal, I note in my diary: '*'Rwy'n dechrau bod yn* embarrassed *o achos bod fi'n smelo o chwys, ond 'rwy'n anghofio defnyddio'r stuff*' ('I'm starting to feel embarrassed because I smell of sweat, but I forget to use the stuff [meaning deodorant]'). I'm a skinny, flat-chested child but decide, on 16 January: '*Mae tamed bach o dyfiant ar* chest *fi*' ('There's a little bit of growth on my chest'). This is a great relief, given that both boys and girls are obsessed with the novelty of breasts. By July, Eryl buys me my first bra from Mackross. My bust is all of 27 inches. D— J— asks me if my periods have started. Secretly pleased, I tell him to mind his own business.

The pressure to work at home intensifies and I'm discouraged from going out. It's now half term:

> *Mi weithies i trwy'r dydd ac 'rwy'n ffed up. Mae 'ngwddwg i dal yn dost. Yn y prynhawn, fe ffoniodd L— D— fi i ofyn os gallen i fynd gyda hi i werthu rhaglenni y 'The Merchant of Venice' ond nid oedd Mam yn fodlon. 'Rwy'n* sick *o weithio … Mi fues i yn y tŷ ar ben fy hunan bron trwy'r dydd.*
>
> (I worked all day and I'm fed up. My throat's still sore. In the afternoon, L— D— phoned me to ask if I could go with her to sell the 'Merchant of Venice' programmes, but Mam wasn't willing. I'm sick of working … I was in the house on my own nearly all day.)
>
> (26 February 1973)

I'm still unhappy the following day:

> *Mi weithies i trwy'r dydd ar y traethawd Cymraeg, ac 'rwy wedi gwneud tua 12–13 ochr. 'Rwy'n* totally fed up – *hwn yw'r gwyliau mwyaf* miserable *ges i erioed.*

> (I worked all day on the Welsh essay, and I've done about 12–13 sides. I'm totally fed up – this is the most miserable holiday I ever had.)
>
> (27 February 1973)

By now, the misery at home is so entrenched that I'm too dispirited to explain the details of its occasions.

It's hard to convey how little I have to do to provoke a reprimand: '*Yn y nos, fe watches i* "Carry on Doctor" *yn lle gweithio ac mae Mam wedi cael siom ynof fi*' ('In the night, I watched "Carry on Doctor" instead of working and Mam is disappointed in me'). I'm thirteen years old and need a laugh. Eryl's constant chivvying of me to do more, do better, shows a total lack of trust. Left to my own devices, I would have done well at school anyway. I like the work and enjoy using my brain. I don't mind being known as a 'swot' because that's what I am. My schoolmates don't give me a hard time in general about being top or near the top of the class because I'm willing to help them. For example, a friend had forgotten to write a poem about a butterfly for an assignment, so I knock one up for her during break. In Latin, the boy I sit next to (and flirt with) is copying my Latin, so I show the instinct of a future freelance writer:

> *Yn Lladin fe aeth D— J— â nodiadir [sic] fi i gopïo cyfieithiad – 'rwy'n mynd i chargo 1c am bob paragraph.*
>
> (In Latin D— J— took my notebook to copy a translation – I'm going to charge 1p for every paragraph.)
>
> (14 September 1973)

As if the pressure to perform academically weren't already too much, Rhydfelen's emphasis on the *eisteddfod* aspect of Welsh culture, combined with Eryl's obsession with writing for competition at home, make me even more wretched. The annual St David's Day school *eisteddfod* at the beginning of March pits four 'houses' or teams against each other, so that individual competition contributes towards an overall house win. I don't write my diary for the Christmas holiday of 1972, perhaps because I'm too busy being 'encouraged' to compose multiple entries for the literary competitions.

Friday, 2 March 1973 is my first *eisteddfod* day at Rhydfelen and my industriousness over Christmas bears fruit. I'm embarrassed now to read of my entry:

> *Mi ennilles i'r unawd piano, 1af, 2ail a 3ydd yn y barddoniaeth Saesneg. Cydradd gyntaf mewn un adrodd, ac ail yn y llall, 3ydd yn y cerdd dant (nid wy'n cofio rhagor) ... Mi GES I'R GADAIR A'R CWPAN PENCAMPWR.*
>
> (I won the piano solo, 1st, 2nd and 3rd in the English poetry. Joint first in one recitation, second in the other, 3rd in the cerdd dant[10] (I don't remember more) ... I HAD THE CHAIR AND THE CHAMPION'S CUP.)
>
> (2 March 1973)

The lower school champion's cup is a huge silver trophy which I have difficulty dragging home on the school bus. But, I win a lot of points for my house, Dinefwr, which carries the day. I hate the sound of my own name being announced: 'GWYNETHLEWIS!' is a creature I don't want to be. Others, who aren't receiving their dues in the written competitions because 'GWYNETHLEWIS!' is so dominant, are understandably frustrated. Pupils are kind when they could have been mean. As I go for my lunch, voices call out congratulations and I smile modestly – no, I grimace – which gives me a name for not being a bighead.

The only competition among these that pleases me is the Chair, which is a big deal for a poet. With the Crown, it's one of the two major prizes in the poetry world, dating back to early medieval poetry competitions, when bards were apprenticed to masters in order to gain a licence to be court poets. Reinvented in the eighteenth century, each St David's Day school *eisteddfod*

10 Singing a lyric in counter-tune to the harp.

(or 'sitting') mimics the convocation of poets who decide on those worthy to be a Prifardd ('Chief Bard'). My feelings are hopelessly mixed. I want to be a poet, but this way of doing it is tainted. Eryl has pushed me to compete too much and is also 'editing' my work to a degree that makes me uncomfortable.

In 1973, I'm mortified by an essay that appears under my name in the school magazine, *Na N'og*, which collects the 'best' writing from the whole school. The piece is entitled '*Rhwng Gwyll a Gwawr*' ('Between Dusk and Dawn') and is about my not being able to fall

Gwyneth with *eisteddfod* trophy, 1973

asleep the instant my head hits the pillow. I trace the impressions of the day but then comes a sentence which made me squirm then and now:

> *Yn araf iawn, fe ddaw pethau mwy dychmygol i'm meddwl. Efallai, os gweithiaf yn galed, mi allaf ennill pob cystadleuaeth yn y mabolgampau a dod yn arwres yr holl ysgol …*
>
> (Very gradually, more imaginary things come to my mind. Perhaps, if I work hard, I can win *every* competition in the sports and become heroine for the whole school.)

I'm not athletic. I'm a good swimmer but I don't compete because it makes me too nervous. Team sports, throwing things and running make no sense to me. However, Eryl and my sister were both athletic. I now wonder if Eryl was fantasising one omnicompetent, composite daughter, an amalgam of us three. When, rightly, I'm teased for that sentence on the bus, I can say nothing in my own defence without implicating my mother, which I can't do, out of loyalty. Stay silent and I'm presenting a sham self to the world – what's more, one I don't like. The double bind makes me hot with shame.

—*What did Eryl want from me?*
—*Herself.*

Ironically, during my teen years, Eryl was making her own way as a writer and experiencing success. She begins to write short stories for children and adults. BBC television and radio producers clearly like her work and she's in demand:

> *Yn y prynhawn, fe aeth Mam i weld Evelyn Williams, ac fe gaethon nhw chat hir. Mae Miss Williams am i Mam drosi unrhyw stori neu lyfr Saesneg i'r Gymraeg.*

Y mae Bernard Evans wedi derbyn y stori i 'Dywedwch chi', ac yn y nos, fe ffoniodd rhyw ddyn i ofyn i Mam i ysgrifennu stori arall.

(In the afternoon, Mam went to see Evelyn Williams and they had a long chat. Miss Williams wants Mam to translate any story or book in English into Welsh. Bernard Evans has accepted the story for 'You say', and in the night, some man phoned to ask Mam to write another story.)

(2 February 1972)

In 1975, she begins to compete in local *eisteddfodau* in her own right:

Fe en[n]illodd Mam y delyneg a chael yr ail wobr am stori fer yn Nhreganna! Great*! ... Fe enillodd Mam yr ail am y gadair ... – ail! Rwy'n* chuffed.

(Mam won the lyric and had second prize for a short story in Treganna! Great! ... Mam won second for the chair ... – second! I'm chuffed.)

(23–4 February 1975)

I'm genuinely thrilled with her success, but this isn't entirely an unselfish emotion. A happy Eryl takes the pressure off me. On 2 April, '*Fe ysgrifennodd Mam delyneg a soned – mae'n nhw'n dda*' ('Mam wrote a lyric and a sonnet – they're good'). In April that year, at the Eisteddfod y Fro ('the Regional Eisteddfod') at Barry College, I win fifty pence for recitation and Eryl wins 'lots' of literary prizes. I hang outside the hall for a lot of the time with a gang of friends from school '*yn chwerthin tan ein bod ni'n sâl*' ('laughing till we were sick').

—That's more like it. Eryl inside, winning, you outside the hall, having fun.

That year, I enjoy 'a good Christmas', as my parents give me a typewriter, the best present ever. My sister gives me a pair of false eyelashes which I love, though I can't do them justice.

Spending time out and about with Eryl, focused on something else other than my shortcomings, gives a tantalising glimpse of what a mother-daughter relationship could be. My idea of a good day doesn't need to involve any special activity. 26 July 1973 is a happy, relaxed day:

> *Dyma ddiwrnod braf cyntaf y gwyliau. Yn gynnar mi orffenes i 'Lord of the Rings'. Yna fe aethon ni lan i Newbridge i gael spring i'r 'fan'. Yna fe gawson ni ein cinio ar y Banne. Fe aethon ni trwy gwlad pert iawn cyn cyrraedd mynydd (2,005 tr). Fe ddringon ni lan i'r top (gan bigo llysiau duon bach ar y ffordd). Ar y ffordd lawr fe welson ni darddiad afon – 'roedd e'n oer ofnadwy ac yn blasu'n great. Hefyd ar y ffordd lawr dyma fi, mam a Marian yn eistedd ar ein penolion a llithro lawr mewn steil. Diwrnod pleserus iawn – buddiol mewn mwy nag un ffordd.*
>
> (This was the first fine day of the holiday. Early on, I finished 'Lord of the Rings'. Then we went up to Newbridge to get a spring for the 'van' [Dad's car]. Then we had our lunch on the Beacons. We went through very pretty countryside before reaching a mountain (2,005 ft). We climbed up to the top (picking bilberries on the way). On the way down we saw a river's source – it was very cold and tasted great. Also on the way down I, mam and Marian sat on our bottoms and slid down in style. A very pleasurable day – profitable in more than one way.)

All I need to thrive is to see Eryl enjoying life and sharing that with us. That summer, we go to stay for a week in Llanddewi

Brefi on a friend's farm, and visit Anti Marged Jane in Talgarreg. Our favourite pastime is playing crazy golf on the Aberystwyth prom. Later that summer, Eryl takes us to visit the Roman ruins at Bath and the Costume Museum, with its *tableaux vivants* showing the development of fashion by the decade since the nineteenth century. Most exciting, we visit Laura Ashley's new shop and I leave with a brown full-length dress with cap sleeves. On 21 August, we go to check out Carrefour, the first hypermarket to come to south Wales, a great novelty at the time. My diary notes that it was 'very nice' and I buy some Johnson's baby soap. It takes so little to make things right for me and yet, most of the time, it seems impossible.

Another reason that summer is contented is that Eryl and I are working on an Herbarium. The brief is to collect plants with medicinal uses and to outline how they've been used in treatment. We consult the work of herbalists such as the seventeenth-century Nicholas Culpeper and the Meddygon Myddfai (the Doctors of Myddfai). We use the English names in order to identify specimens from numerous textbooks but the final project uses only the Latin and Welsh. It's for yet another *eisteddfod* competition, which we don't win, but this work sparks a lifelong delight in botany for me.

Before starting, we visit the wax flowers that used to be on public display in the National Museum of Wales. These models fascinate me because not only are they accurate depictions of plant specimens, they're works of art. The curator of this department shows us how to press plants in blotting paper placed under heavy books and then to mount them on stiff card with the correct butterfly tape. The weather is good and we collect specimens from a variety of terrains in south Wales, including the old canal that brought coal and steel down to Cardiff from the south Wales valleys. We spend a particularly memorable day on Kenfig dunes, where we find the hairy-leaved and vividly named Viper's Bugloss.

At the time, it escapes my attention that the names for herbs are all related to pain. The text that Eryl and I write is a catalogue of the body's vulnerability to harm. The entries in my handwriting next to the pressed plants evoke all those who have been poisoned, suffer rheumatism, retain water, have been burned or endured bloody noses and wounds. But there's no diagnosis or treatment for the harm in which we're living.

The poisonous plants fascinate me in particular. Soon, I learn to identify the purple and yellow pointed flowers of common nightshade or bittersweet, and I see it everywhere – on waste ground, growing out of cracks in brickwork and, even, cultivated out of ignorance in gardens. I feel anxious for unwitting children and pets surrounded by such attractive hazards.

Deadly nightshade (*atropa belladonna*) is the most notorious member of the Solanaceae family. It's rumoured that, combined with opium poppy, monkshood and hemlock, deadly nightshade was used in witches' flying ointment, a stimulant for hallucinatory dreaming and aids to contacting the spirit world. I long to collect such a potent aid to the imagination. Used as a recreational drug it's doubly dangerous because atropine penetrates the blood-brain barrier. In the past, the substance was used in ophthalmology to dilate the pupils for surgery but is now considered too toxic for the purpose. Nightshade's effect of slowing the movement of the gut make it useful in chemical warfare, one toxin mitigating the effect of another. In the early 2000s, when Leighton and I went sailing long-distance, my favourite sea-sickness remedy was a scopolamine patch stuck behind the ear. This drug is derived from deadly nightshade, so I know the hazards of overdosing well and cut up my patches into halves and quarters, in order to avoid eye problems. I notice now how closely the effects of belladonna poisoning echo a migraine attack: sensitivity to light, blurred vision, tachycardia, loss of balance, staggering, headache, rash, flushing, severely dry mouth and throat, slurred speech, urinary retention, constipation, confusion, hallucinations, delirium. I can see myself now, lying in bed on a sunny day. The pupils of my brain are dilated, blinding me, so my hands cover my face in the universal gesture of shame.

The Welsh name for deadly nightshade is *ceirios y Gŵr Drwg* ('the Devil's cherries') and refers to its fruit which are so black, shiny and sweet tasting that they can tempt. Three berries are enough to kill a child. In Alnwick Castle's famous Poison Garden, which includes plants from the Solanaceae family, visitors have been known to be overcome by noxious fragrances and have to be dragged out. Writing this book now feels like it's killing me.

—*Your deadly nightshade was growing right next to you.*

Unfortunately, my chance of finding a specimen of *atropa belladonna* in Wales were and are slim, as the plant only grows on a few sites on the coast of Glamorgan and in the Wye valley. I consider this book to be my careful taxonomy and description of the nature, signs, symptoms and uses for my nightshade mother, in whose dark light I have lived, and still do. She is potent, glamorous, hugely beneficial in small quantities and fatal in overdose.

In 1974, Eryl crosses a further line. She notices a set task in the same *eisteddfod*'s embroidery section: to depict a fruit in fabric. I've never done more embroidery than the usual cross-stitch taught in junior school. However, our next-door neighbour, Mrs Evans, teaches textile design at an art college and offers to help. In consultation with her, Eryl draws the section of a tomato (known in Welsh as an *afal cariad* – 'love apple') and, under Mrs Evans's direction, produces a complex piece of art which conveys the texture of the fruit. Knot stitch in a variety of sizes and colours depict shade, layered net in a collage distinguishes between the pulp and the juice of the tomato, while a rich variety of buttons and beads stand for the seeds. It's wonderful work and not one bit of it is mine. I'm not even allowed to touch it, for fear of spoiling it. Eryl submits the piece under my name and is awarded a prize. She then hangs the work on the sitting-room wall. I can't bear to look at it because it reminds me of the fraud.

It's impossible for me to alert anybody. Here's an adult submitting her own work as that of her child, a strange kind of impersonation. Why on earth didn't she enter an embroidery competition under her own name? What could possibly be the gratification in passing your own work off as that of a teenager? The Welsh word for this action is 'tadogi' which, according to *Geiriadur Prifysgol Cymru* ('University of Wales Dictionary') means to 'father, beget, create; determine paternity of (child), affiliate, trace etymology of'. My mother was fathering a piece of art on me, a bizarre psychodrama. I can only think that it was masochistic on Eryl's part – not receiving credit for her own work – but also a form of cowardice. Here was a way of competing which posed no risk to her publicly, because any failure would be ascribed to me. Nor was she competing with her equals. Or was this bizarre behaviour creating, in her mind, a 'Gwyneth' who would be acceptable to her? Was she recasting herself as me, fantasising that she'd had my opportunities in life? Was the true thrust of her pretence that I was to lend her my name – and, increasingly, my life – to make up for the unfairness that she'd undoubtedly experienced as a child? If so, our relationship depended entirely on the degree to which I consented to be her creature.

There's no word that I know to describe the kind of abuse that involves hijacking another person's capacity for creating art. Since leaving home, I've learned to avoid such people at all costs. As a child, though, I was in Château Despair and the doors were locked.

My distress takes on a new twist when I develop a fear of burglars entering my bedroom window, which is over the flat roof of a sun lounge. Climbing up would have been easy. I terrify myself with a fantasy of violent entry – not hard to decode sexually. Gwilym rigs up a way of wedging the double glazing ajar, making it secure. On 23 June 1974, I'm again obsessing about not having done enough homework, working on maths and history all day, convinced that I'll fail tests (I never did).

I'm finding it hard to sleep. I'd listen to the transistor radio my parents had given me in bed. I love the voices so intimate in my ear. It's like eavesdropping from the womb, evidence that there's a different world out there. When this doesn't work, Eryl tries another strategy: '*Rhoddodd Mam* antihistamine *i fi i gysgu'n iawn ac anghofio am y lladron y tu allan*' ('Mam gave me antihistamine for me to sleep properly and to forget about the thieves outside').

—*The burglar was already inside the house.*
—*Antihistamine isn't a stupid idea … If I ever can't sleep …*
—*She's drugging you instead of listening!*
—*Why didn't you warn me?*
—*I did, but you couldn't hear me then.*

My mother, aided and abetted by my father, was breaking into my life and stealing what wasn't hers – that is, my ability to act in my own interests, without interference from them. The capture of my writing was bad enough but the loss of my own point of view was infinitely more grave. I was being robbed of the uncomfortable but essential process of discerning what I, rather than other people, wanted. This ability to discriminate between various options and choose is that core of the self which takes time and practice to build. I was being bullied into believing that I had no right to a self that could disagree with what my parents wanted. For all Gwilym's emphasis on looking after 'Number One' which I never understood, if you're gaslit out of a self, then that's impossible to put into practice.

—*He had a self but denied you yours.*

I find a fictional specimen of deadly nightshade in a novel, L. P. Hartley's *The Go-Between*. Leo, a boy on the brink of adulthood, spends the summer in a schoolfriend's great house. He still believes in magic and is enthralled when he finds a deadly nightshade growing in a neglected part of the garden:

> But it wasn't a plant, in my sense of the word, it was a shrub, almost a tree, and as tall as I was. It looked the picture of evil and also the picture of health, it was so glossy and strong and juicy-looking: I could almost see the sap rising to nourish it. It seemed to have found the place in all the world that suited it best.

> I knew that every part of it was poisonous, I knew too that it was beautiful … I felt that the plant could poison me, even if I didn't touch it, and that if I didn't eat it, it would eat me, it looked so hungry, in spite of all the nourishment it was getting.

Leo, with the susceptibility of a child, falls in love with Ted, a local farmer, and also with Marian, daughter of the house, with whom Ted is conducting an illicit affair. The two manipulate Leo into acting as a postman for them, carrying notes between them, so that they can keep their liaison secret. In the story, these two elements combine and result in catastrophe for all the characters. The poisonous plant is inert until its action is precipitated by another element.

In our house, when there was any crisis between Eryl and me, Gwilym became our go-between. He'd try to diffuse one party's anger towards the other without ever addressing the cause of the conflict. I was, mainly, to keep my head down and not be angry. How one does that when one's whole existence is being attacked, I shall never know. These crises fell into a pattern. The weekend would arrive and Eryl would find me more annoying than usual because she was exhausted from teaching. My father and sister would make themselves scarce but I would inevitably do something that would set Eryl off into a fury. There'd be recriminations, shouting, slamming doors. I'd flee to my room and Eryl would retreat to hers. I'd hear Gwilym taking a cup of tea to Eryl and talking to her in a soothing voice. There she would rest and ignore us all, often for three days.

Eventually, he'd come to my bedroom and try to soothe me, expressing his frustration with me for being unable to read the signals and for 'setting Mam off'. He'd insist that Eryl was suffering more than anybody. She was, clearly, depressed, but that didn't mean that it was right for her to tyrannise the whole household. Gwilym had nothing to say about the justice of the situation, it was all about appeasing Eryl. To make a wartime analogy, I was a country annexed by an enemy and, instead of protesting, was instructed to accommodate my aggressor by trying harder next time not to give her cause for taking over more of my territory. Gwilym, my sister and I would creep around the house for the remaining time of Eryl's crisis. The atmosphere would be much more relaxed, until we heard the floorboards upstairs creaking, and we'd freeze until she went back to bed and all went quiet again. Eventually, she'd emerge, as if nothing had happened. She never apologised and we were expected to move on without resolving the issue. Thus she never had to deal with any of her behaviour nor admit any responsibility for her actions. I was to blame but I knew that was wrong.

I'd like to think that Gwilym was on my side all along. I'd like to think that he was secretly cheering me on in my rejection of Eryl's campaign to control me while blaming me for the terrible feelings she was experiencing. I'd like to think that he was genuinely trying to steer a middle path between us. Holding Eryl to account for her poisonous behaviour towards me, even as a young child, would have benefitted us all.

—No, he went for the easy life ...
—I still find that difficult to believe.
—Then give me one instance of him siding with you against Eryl.
—To my knowledge, he never did. Not once.

What surprises me also is how little anger I express in the diaries. Now, I lose my temper once a decade and when that happens, people remember the occasion. This doesn't mean that I don't feel rage, only that I've taught myself to inhibit its expression. Being brought up by Eryl meant that her fury always trumped mine. Any protest on my part made her anger ten times worse, so I learned to stifle my reactions and, if I had to, go to my room and punch a pillow.

Living with Eryl was like sharing a cage with a wild animal. For a while, things would be normal and I'd be lulled into a false sense of security and lower my guard. But, move too suddenly and there it was, the savagery again, ready to maul me.

Many years later, Leighton and I tried to adopt a feral cat who called by our house sometimes for food. He was extremely hostile and, when we tried to touch him, lashed out and drew blood. One day, Charlie (as we'd christened him) called by when Eryl was visiting. Before we could warn her about the cat's nature, she stroked him and he gave himself up in purring ecstasy at her touch. Were we seeing two wild characters recognising each other? From then on, Leighton nicknamed my mother 'Feral Eryl'.

—Mwnci, I can't be angry with an animal.
—But you can, and should be, with a mother.

As I slog through my diaries, I want to shout at my younger self not to internalise Eryl's character assassination of me. On 11 April 1974, I'm in trouble for what seems a trivial infraction: '*Mam yn grac oherwydd i fi wisgo trowsus a oedd wedi eu golchi'n ddiweddar*' ('Mam angry because I wore trousers that had been recently washed'). I'm concerned: '*Hoffen i pe bawn i'n gallu gwneud rhywbeth wir i helpu*' ('I'd like it if I could do something to really help'). The only other person who understands how bad things are is my sister, and she's so busy trying to keep out of trouble herself that we're unable to make an alliance against Eryl. By now, she's come to teach in Rhydfelen, so she has seniority in that territory as well.

I can't imagine that I'm any worse than other teenagers of my background. I'd tried to show sympathy about Eryl's exhaustion, but have been swiftly rebuffed:

> *Fe ddywedodd Mam wrthyf fi i beidio a bod yn sofft pan ofynnes i iddi os oedd hi wedi blino. Mae'n treial caledi [sic] fi, yn ôl hi.*
>
> (Mam told me not to be soft when I asked her if she was tired. She's trying to harden me, according to her.)
>
> (30 October 1974)

One moment I'm being reproached for being selfish, the next for being soft. And who reproaches a child for expressing concern? Who wants to harden a child? The final phrase of this entry – 'according to her' – shows that I'm beginning to distinguish between Eryl's point of view and my own.

By the second month into the 1974 academic year I'm at my wits' end again. Eryl and I had been to town on the glamorous assignment of buying dressing gowns in Marks & Spencer:

> *Yn y prynhawn, fe ddechreues i wban am y gwaith, ac fe aeth Mam yn upset ofnadwy oherwydd fy mod i'n ffanatic. Beth yw e fy mod i'n cymeryd drwy'r amser, a byth yn rhoi dim.*
>
> (In the afternoon, I started sobbing about the work, and Mam became very upset because I'm a fanatic. What is it that I take all the time, and never give anything.)
>
> (9 November 1974)

How come my distress has been upstaged by Eryl's upset and morphed into a discussion about my selfishness? Cowed, I note that, in the night, I get on with studying the agricultural revolution for a history test.

Rows happen with increasing frequency. Almost at random I pick out this entry: '*Mam yn grac a fi heddiw – rwy'n gwybod fy mod i'n ei haeddu ond …*' ('Mam angry with me today – I know that I deserve it but …') On Boxing Day, Eryl's telling me where I'm going wrong and, the same night, there's a further explosion. Next day, I have another telling off. I rarely mention what I've done because it doesn't matter. Eryl's reaction to me is the only opinion that count.

My ego is systematically being destroyed. There are a number of entries expressing self-hatred, such as this on 14 January 1974: '*Ma cymeriad hunanol ac isel ofnadwy 'da fi. Ych.*' ('I have a selfish and very low character. Yuk.') The theme is repeated ad nauseam, like this entry on 19 May 1974: '*Rwy'n hen beth diog, hunanol,* vain, self-illusioned a bigheaded' ('I'm a lazy, selfish, vain, self-illusioned and bigheaded old thing').

I watch my self-hatred deepen:

> *Yn y nos, dechrau ar y daearyddiaeth. Mae'n ymddangos i fi fy mod i'n ryw* swotty, square scarecrow *yn yr ysgol … 'Does dim ynni gen i i wenu a bod yn ffraeth, fel mae'r merched eraill, ac 'rwy'n hyll dros ben ymhob ffordd.*
>
> (In the night, start on the geography. It seems to me that I'm some kind of swotty, square scarecrow in school … I don't have any energy to smile and be witty, like the other girls, and I'm very ugly in every way.)
>
> (17 January 1975)

Compared to the treatment I'm enduring at home, any teasing at school seems like nothing. One day, I'm standing outside the school library when a giant of a boy in a class above me says, loudly, that some people were getting poets to write *eisteddfod* poems for them. The bully had sensed that there was something odd going on, but hadn't quite identified the full extent of the problem. I was both the actual poet writing prize-winning entries and also the person whose name was being used to present work that wasn't all mine.

Far from relaxing her vigilance for mistakes on my part as I grow older, it seemed to me that Eryl's rage with me becomes ever more unreasonable. I like school dinners, which we pay for with small green pieces of paper that resemble raffle tickets. I'm already fifteen when my diary notes:

> *Yn y nos, cael row ofnadwy am docynnau cinio. 'Rown i wedi eu colli ddydd Llun, ac yn lle mynd i ofyn i mam am arian, fe es i i dalu allan o'n arian i fy hun. Yn hytrach na mynd âg £1 i'r ysgol mi ofynnes i i mam am y 50p yr oedd hi'n ddyledus i fi.*
>
> (At night, had a terrible row about lunch tokens. I had lost them on Monday, and instead of going to ask mam for money, I went to pay out of my own money.

> Rather than take £1 to school [making change was difficult when buying tokens] I asked mam for the 50p that was owing me.)
>
> (10 July 1975)

I'm taking responsibility for my own mistake and don't expect Eryl to pay. I want to use my own money but even that isn't acceptable.

The gloom has intensified significantly by December 1975. I'm sixteen when I write:

> *Yn y nos, mi ddes i adre'n teimlo'n hollol ddiflas – a chael row am fod yn* cheeky. *Mi es i lan llofft a chael dim te … 'Rwy'n hollol ffed up o bawb, a 'dwy jyst ddim yn gwybod sut i feddwl am fy hunan – bod yn llawn hunan-hyder, poeni am neb – yna cael fy ngalw'n* selfish *– neu* soft *a Mam yn gwneud hwyl ar fy mhen i.*
>
> (In the night, I came home feeling totally miserable – and had a row for being cheeky. I went upstairs and had no tea … I'm totally fed up of everybody, and I just don't know how to think about myself – to be full of self-confidence, not worrying about anybody – then being called selfish – or soft and Mam making fun of me.)
>
> (11 December 1975)

From these tirades, you would never have guessed that my marks were exemplary (except for maths).

In similar vein:

> *Ar ôl dod adref, cael pryd o dafod gan Mam am fod yn ddiog a hunanol, sy'n berffaith wir. 'Rwy'n cwyno am bethau, ond 'rwy'n rhy ddiog i wneud unrhywbeth amdanyn nhw.*

> (After coming home, I'm given a tongue-lashing by Mam for being lazy and selfish, which is perfectly true. I complain about things, but I'm too lazy to do anything about them.)
>
> (4 February 1976)

—Tell me Munci, was I lazy and selfish?
—You were not.

When our class holds a 1976 New Year's fancy-dress party in Tito's nightclub in town, it's an irony not lost on me now that I go as a rag doll, in a red dress, my hair in bunches tied with ribbons and stripy socks. Like Raggedy-Ann, the doll Eryl made for me as a child, the smile has been torn off my face and only a smudge of glue remains to show where it had been. I feel like my mother's punchbag.

The pressure to continue winning in art competitions intensifies. For the school *eisteddfod* in 1974, I write thirteen literary competition pieces. In 1975, this increases to nineteen written entries. During the Christmas holidays, the big issue is, again, writing. I'm still willing to go along with Eryl's 'encouragements':

> *Mae Mam am i fi ennill y Gadair a'r dlws [sic] Saesneg yn yr eisteddfod* – personal ambition *hi. Wel, mi ga' i go.*
>
> Mam wants me to win the Chair and the English Trophy – her personal ambition. Well, I'll give it a go.
>
> (2 January 1977)

It's so hard not to despise myself now for giving in.

—It wasn't your fault, Gwyn, you were a hostage.

I did win the *eisteddfod* chair, but that no longer gives me pleasure. In my diary, I note: ‘‘*rwy wir yn casáu'r seremoni yna*’ (‘I really hate that ceremony’), though I do appreciate the ‘*corn gwlad*’ (the ‘country horn’, or in this case Fiona Bennet's trumpet) that summons the winning bard to stand up in the crowd and the comedy of becoming entangled in the gown worn by the Archdruid Reynolds (the religious studies teacher). After this, I'm so depressed, so worn down by the conflicts at home, that I more or less stop keeping my beloved diary. The same year, I win the Literature Medal at the Urdd National Eisteddfod. The best thing about that was that the Urdd publishes my first pamphlet.

The results of these contradictory feelings about writing have stayed with me. I've wanted success (as if my life depended on it) but have also feared it (as a sign of over-compliance with other people's standards), leaving me paralysed. The nautical term is being in irons, when one sail has flipped to one side of the boat while the other, on the opposite side, is working against it. The boat has no purchase on the wind and, wallowing, goes nowhere.

The following year I tell Eryl that I'm not going to compete in the school *eisteddfod* at all. She does everything in her emotional blackmail repertoire but, for the first time, I won't budge. My diary is blank for this period, always a sign of unhappiness. I remember her saying to me:

‘*Fydd y berthynas rhyngddon ni byth yr un peth ar ôl hyn.*’

(‘The relationship between us will never be the same after this.’)

As far as I'm concerned, that can only be a good thing.

ANTIDOTES

I do not like her. She doth think she has
Strange ling'ring poisons: I do know her spirit;
And will not trust one of her malice with
A drug of such damn'd nature … She is fool'd
With most false effect: and I the truer,
So be false with her.

(Shakespeare, *Cymbeline*)

Chapter 6

TWO KINDS OF ELSEWHERE

In his definition of the word 'antidote', the medieval etymologist Isidore of Seville – whose derivations are often imaginary, but always stimulating – offers two contradictory ways of looking at the word. The first traces its root from the Latin '*antidotum* [which] means derived (*datum*) from the opposite ... for opposites are cured by opposites in accordance with the methodology of medicine.'

—Mwnci, tell me what is the antidote to a nightshade mother?
—Love differently, love elsewhere.

It wasn't till the summer that I was sixteen that I saw a way of surviving a toxic upbringing.

A knee injury had stopped me from taking part in sports for a number of years and, unable to find an answer in the UK, Eryl kindly sent me to America to visit my aunt, Megan, in the hope that she, a paediatrician, could diagnose and treat the injury. Megan and Bill Tanner meet me in O'Hare airport, Chicago, producing juice and Welsh cakes before we drive the 200 miles south to Bill's hometown, Danville, Illinois. The epitome of small-town America, Danville is the birthplace of Dick Van Dyke and Gene Hackman. An outing to the Custard Cup (still in its 1950s décor) for an ice cream is an event of a summer evening and the air-conditioned mall holds such delights as JC Penney, and a stall selling Fannie May chocolates, one to be eaten every night before bed.

Bill and Megan live just outside town at Hafod y Coed, a redbrick farmhouse. 'Hafod' in Welsh refers to the high pastures to which sheep are taken during the summer. The house name, therefore, means 'Summer Grazing of the Trees', as if the woods were a herd of livestock. Inside, the house is suffused with a chlorophyll light.

We mention the knee briefly at the beginning of my visit and then have such a good time together that we forget all about it. Spending time with Megan, though, helps me to identify a much deeper malaise in my life and a possible way forward for me.

It's a summer of great forces. On my first morning, I'm still jet-lagged, so Bill and Megan leave me to sleep. I'm alone in the house with the two rescue dogs, Betsy and Thunder. I'm woken suddenly at two in the afternoon by a thunderclap right over the house. Betsy, an Alsatian, is cowering, shivering by the side of my bed, and the room is bathed in uncanny storm light, like a scene from *The Wizard of Oz*. The dog's fear makes me brave so, in pelting rain and still in my nightdress, we both run through the storm's violence next door to the Huckstadts' house. Megan finds me there later, having made friends with Suzie, who's my own age, and eating chilli con carne for the first time, astonished that you're meant to crumble your crackers into the stew. That storm is a gateway into a world of different family dynamics and one of the happiest, most important months of my life.

We fall into a pattern. During the week, when Bill and Megan are working, I'm left to my own devices. For the first time ever, nobody's at me, telling me what to do. I discover a record player and listen to Tchaikovsky and Beethoven symphonies. Megan notices that I like Danish pastries and buys me Bear Claws for breakfast. In four weeks, I put on seven pounds, an achievement of which I'm very proud. She gives me old sports T-shirts, hand-me-downs from my five male cousins, worn so often that they're soft and comfortable.

Before I go out into the Hafod y Coed woods, Bill warns me about poison ivy and poison oak, showing me their oily copper-coloured leaves. I'm not confident in my ability to distinguish between the benign and the toxic plants, so I try to remember not to roll around naked in general greenery. Even more worrying to me are chiggers, tiny creatures that, I'm told, can be picked up from skin contact with grass. At the time, we believed that the *Trombiculidae* mite burrows under the skin and remained buried there. It's now known that it 'only' inserts its feeding structure, injecting an enzyme that rots the host's flesh, thus feeding the parasite. Either way, the result is a nasty red rash. Every time I wade into vegetation, I soak my legs in the bathtub afterwards and 'drown' the invaders. Then there are snakes, so I try to be careful about where I put my feet. Wales, with its benign natural world, is highly toxic to me while, ironically, America, with its poisonous plants, skunks, porcupines, snakes, leeches and ticks, gives me a place to recover from being poisoned at home.

The pond is the centre of my days, omphalos of my summer. It isn't a natural body of water. Bill dammed up one of the property's streams so that the family, who are all good swimmers, has a place to bathe. The door to the back porch, on which a chain of brass bells is hung, jangles as it closes behind me. It's never locked. The porch holds the hot fug of dog. At the slam of the screen door, Betsy and Thunder run ahead of me down the path to the creek. In order to help Bill and Megan, I collect water from the spring on my way to the wooded valley. I carry down empty milk cartons and wedge one with its lip in the rivulet to fill, so that I can pick it up on my way back.

It takes so little to make a path – a skirt brushing aside a blade of grass, a dog's tread on trillium – all these contacts, however light, contribute to making a way. As I walk, I clock the plants in flower – there's shining bedstraw – as if I'm pressing them in my mind. The act of noticing them is, in itself, a herbal remedy. A little attention, bestowed lovingly and often, opens up a space through which I and others can travel.

I jump over the creek and climb the opposite slope, with its sycamores, maples and hickories. The morning is loud with crickets and birds. I approach the pond with stealth, so that I can catch it unawares. The dogs and I settle on the dock and I sit with my feet in the water, partly pleased, partly repulsed by the fish that come to nibble and taste my skin. I hear the dry-paper whirr of darners, some coupled, landing on water lily pads and calamus.

I lower myself gingerly into the water, through the scum and bulrushes and out, as quickly as I can, to the clear water. As I move, I feel convection currents of warmth and cold as the water circulates. I imagine these different layers of water as silk scarves in red, orange and indigo. Moving through these textiles is sensuous. The pond is alive and my legs tingle as creatures brush against them. The goal is to reach the raft moored in the middle and sit there for a while, sunning myself.

I'm told that there are snapping turtles here, though I've never seen one. *Chelydra serpentina* is snake-like because of its highly mobile neck. On land, it's aggressive and possesses beak-like jaws, rumoured to be capable of biting a finger off a human hand. In water, it's likely to avoid contact and hide under the surface in sediment. This doesn't comfort me at all and the nerves in my lower limbs tingle with anticipated pain every time I enter the pond. Snapping turtles can live as long as a century. I imagine mine as a solitary female, lurking with intent. The moment I'm distracted by pleasure, she'll fix her mighty jaws on my thigh and drag me down into the cold bottom. I push that terror away, as I'm determined that an imaginary monster isn't going to deter me from what's become a ritual. I have to see the pond daily and swim in it. Years later, my cousin Joe confides that the boys all worried about another part of their anatomy in the pond and, so, swam a lot of backstroke.

Sometimes I'm joined by Bill, who looks like Glenn Miller, and never abandons his GI buzz cut and wire-rimmed glasses. He has a sly sense of humour and the Midwesterner's leisurely approach to conversation. He teases me about being 'a social butterfly' (all as a result of the parties he and Megan have arranged for me to attend) and I love him for it. Bill's quiet exterior hides a core of steel. After qualifying as a doctor, he served in the medical corps of the US Navy and was assigned to the Marines, running an aid station on Iwo Jima. He was treating a casualty on one of the smaller islands during that campaign and looked up, momentarily, to see the last Navy boat departing. Fortunately, someone remembered him and came back.

Various of my five blonde cousins drift home for a few days and then depart. There's a rope hanging from one of the trees above the pond and it's a family initiation rite to swing on it, over the water, dropping into the pond. It takes me the whole summer to pluck up the courage but when Tom, my youngest cousin, is visiting, female pride dictates that I do it, once.

One evening, I'm up at the pond and Megan and Bill, back from work, find me in the water. It's been a scorcher. Without giving it a second thought, Megan takes off her work skirt and blouse and, wearing only bra and pants, joins me in the water. Seeing this, I conceive an ambition: to be a middle-aged woman who thinks nothing of stripping off to swim in a pond. And I am.

Megan introduces me to birdwatching. She and Bill keep a bird table and teach me to identify its visitors. Red cardinal is easy to remember, as is bluejay, as are chickadees, smaller and cheekier than sparrows at home. My favourites are the extravagant flickers.

One evening, Bill calls me out to see the Milky Way. Another time, it's to watch the firefly constellations. I'm offered so many wonders that my imagination is fired. Nothing is expected in return. Bill and Megan like me, which is a bigger deal than being loved. At home, the love that is undoubtedly there brings me only anguish and distress. Here, I bathe in a kindness that keeps a respectful distance. I can breathe.

To give me an idea of the area, Bill and Megan take me for a spin in their aeroplane. We drive to the local airfield and out of a hangar's maw emerges a single-engine Bonanza – the Blue Goose. I step up carefully onto the wing, clamber into the back. Bill talks to the tower, works through a checklist, calmly flicking switches and noting dials. Megan settles down in the front seat with her knitting. For Bill and Megan, flying is no different from going out in the car for an evening spin. We taxi along the runway, then the bumping stops as we're lifted into the uneven air. It's been a scorching day and we feel columns of heat rise from the fields and roads, rocking the plane. I think that we might be about to die, but it's worth it.

In the back of the Blue Goose, I relax and look down at Danville. The plains are a physical shock to my hill-oriented Welsh brain. If there are no mountains against which to push, how will your mind ever stop expanding? The plains stretch endlessly, with the silent letters of Illinois. Later in life, I learn to live beyond the terms set by Eryl-as-opposition, so that I'm not simply fuelled by defiance, which would have been no liberation at all, but it takes a very long time to accumulate the escape velocity needed to gain the distance to make my own choices. I observe everything and draw my own conclusions about the difference between the boys' upbringing and my own.

At night, Hafod y Coed is surrounded by uncanny whip-poor-will calls. Bill and I often listen to them together in the dark before turning in. One of the nightjar or goatsucker family, the bird nests on the ground. The call is onomatopoeic: 'Whip Poor Will!' I'm singing it for you now, the tonic for Whip, down for Poor (ah, self-pity) then a top C for Will – though you whip me, I will! I envisage each enchanting call graphically, like a Greek-letter or a tremolo uptick. Far from being a masochist bird, commanding that Will be whipped (is Will the bird? or another unfortunate?), the song casts doubt on the incitement to violence because it's a question.

My eldest cousin Jim tells me a story that summer which has stayed in my mind. He says that at the beginning of each night, the whip-poor-will hunts for insects on the wing, using its moustache hairs to sense its prey. At dawn, it returns to its ground nest. As a teenager Jim once decided that he had to find the bird's nest so, clutching a torch, he tracks one bird's cries from outside the house. As the night hours pass, Jim narrows the distance between him and the bird. He crosses the creek, carefully placing his feet, moving silently, pretending to be night through the firefly universes. Now he's up on the plateau, near the pond, and so close to his quarry that he can hear – or imagine – the bird's syrinx contract before its cry. The dark becomes grainy and Jim's on his hands and knees in the undergrowth. When he can move no closer, he switches on the torch and there, in its beam, catches *Antrostomus vociferos*. Cinerous greys and browns make the nest look like the ashes of a fire. Jim catches himself, a homunculus in the bird's enormous black dark-discerning eye. I now have a print of Audubon's whip-poor-will hunting moths on my wall. For me, the bird has become a principle.

That summer, as now, I'm tracing the river of my family to its troubling source, speech through the dark to the open mouth. Megan has been raised in the same family as Eryl. At home, my mother attributes her hateful behaviour towards me to her upbringing, as if she has no choice in the matter. My great fear is that it's inevitable that I'll be condemned to live in the same fury as besets Eryl. I look at Megan, brought up in the same dark house as her sister – albeit ten years earlier – and conclude that this isn't inevitable.

The impression I'd received from Eryl was that Megan was bathed in a golden light of her parents' favour, but the picture I gather over the summer from her is subtly different. When Megan went to America during the war, she was already engaged to another man but, having met Bill, decided to marry him instead and to stay in the Midwest. Sarah Ann and Ben James were devastated. Megan returned to Llanddewi Brefi briefly after the war and, as soon as he could, Bill joined her in order to meet her parents. It was a disaster. His US Navy-issue boots were coarse leather and, on the first morning, Sarah Ann tried to polish them, which was impossible. This became a focus for her resentment against Bill for taking Megan away. Bill had to leave and, in the post-war transport chaos, the couple was separated for some time. Not long after, Mamgu opened a letter to Megan from Bill. The closest I ever came to hearing Megan raise her voice is when she tells me:

'I'm an old woman now and I still haven't forgiven her.'

Over the years, my grandparents' attitude mellowed and, once the children began to be born, Ben and Sarah Ann went to Danville to visit.

Bill and Megan adore each other. When they're in their late seventies we share a motel suite in Florida for a week and, on my way to the bathroom, I catch a glimpse of them in bed through an open door. Bill is sleeping with his head on Megan's breast. As I pass, she smiles at me.

All too soon, my month in America draws to its close. Eryl has given me travellers' cheques worth fifty pounds, with strict instructions not to spend them all. She's also told me to look for a dress for a National Eisteddfod recitation competition I'm taking part in later that summer. I find a sleeveless tunic, which I love, in rich reds and browns, tied with a sash under the bust, and Megan buys it for me. I protest that she's spoiling me and that she shouldn't spend her money. She proposes a deal: I'm not to worry, as long as I spend all the money Eryl's given me, she'll pay for everything else. I do and she does.

Before I leave, Megan and Bill have a tea party for my birthday, even though it's August and that isn't until November. I'm given a Bicentennial keyring that I never use and an address book so tiny that it's not practical. Bill has a lifetime addiction to 'free gifts' that come with catalogues and is a lavish dispenser of binoculars that don't work, chains that stain your neck. My main gift, however, is glorious: a Kodak instamatic camera, a new lens through which to see my life.

Megan Tanner, Gwyneth and the Mississippi River

At the very last moment before I return to Wales, I dare to ask Megan clumsily, if I'm like my mother. Megan's uncharacteristically vehement:

'You're nothing like her.'

That gives me courage for the next couple of years and the hope, for the first time, that I don't have to live in the bitterness and strain in which I've been raised.

Many years later, I do tell Megan about the horrible situation at home and Eryl's assertion that it's caused by Mamgu's cruelty towards her. In this, Megan's an expert witness, the only one aside from Eryl who knows what it was like to be Sarah Ann's daughter. Megan's answer is emphatic:

'No. Eryl is worse.'

Now that surprises me.

When I get back to Cardiff, Eryl's apoplectic about the money I've spent. Megan and Bill are condemned for having done nothing for my knee, voiding the whole purpose of the visit, as far as Eryl was concerned. Her reaction to my dress is vicious. It's declared 'totally unsuitable' for an *eisteddfod*. In the end, she buys a blouse to go under it and make it more 'modest'. I've bought presents for the family. Whenever my father used to be offered a cup of tea, he'd insist on 'Half a cup!' so I'd bought him a mug that was cut in half vertically. The joke, which had given me pleasure, was dismissed as pointless. Bill and Megan had recommended a series of paperback novels about American history for Eryl and I bought them for her. They're pronounced trash and put away, unread, in the bottom of a bookcase, as if they were pornography. For Eryl, I'd also bought a Holly Hobbie canvas bag displaying the motto 'Friends are for ever'.

Even worse, I've committed high treason by liking Megan. Eryl mocks me, accusing me, with a withering contempt in her voice, of thinking that Megan is 'perfect'. I don't, but I think she's pretty great. For me, it's never a choice between the sisters but Eryl makes it into one and, like anybody who sets herself up in a power game, she loses that love that isn't a right but is earned.

While I'm sleeping off jet lag, my period arrives unexpectedly early and unusually heavy. Blood leaks in a Jackson Pollock spatter onto the sheets. Eryl rages as she tears at the bedding, blaming me for creating work.

The body's eloquent and writes itself large, on sheets, if necessary, and in scarlet:

SOS. SEND HELP.

None comes.

Even though I've been offered a glimpse of hope, I'm still in Eryl's power. Attacks are becoming more heated and sparked by ever more negligible 'offences':

> *Yn y nos, tra 'rown i'n ysgrifennu'r peth i'r ddarlith, fe gamddeallodd Mam fi a mynd yn biserk – roedd hi'n gwrthod yn lân â gadael i fi egluro.*
>
> (In the night, while I was writing the thing for the lecture, Mam misunderstood me and went berserk – she completely refused to let me explain.)
>
> (23 November 1976)

By 1978, my final year at school, home life has become increasingly grim. I'm facing A levels – good grades mean a ticket out – and have sat the entrance exams for Cambridge. The pressure to do nothing but academic work is intense. In March, I note in my diary:

> *Tymheredd ynddo fi o hyd. 'Rwy wedi bod yn ffwl – wedi cymeryd gormod arnaf fy hun – gall fy nghorff i ddim cymeryd gormod. Rhaid i fi fod mwy gofalus o faint 'rwy'n gwneud yn y dyfodol. Mae fy ngwaith*

> *i'n mwy pwysig. 'Rwy'n gwneud gormod o bethau cymdeithasol – rhaid i fi dorri lawr.*
>
> (Still have a temperature. I've been a fool – have taken too much on myself – my body can't take too much. I have to be more careful about how much I do in the future. My work is more important. I do too many social things – I have to cut down.)
>
> (9 March 1977)

I can't help feeling that I'm parroting my parents in this entry. I needed more of a social life, not less.

Throughout this period, I'm writing repeatedly that I'm overwhelmed: '*Mae popeth yn ormod i fi*' ('Everything's too much for me'); '*rwy'n boddi*' ('I'm drowning'). On 30 January 1978 I say: '*Rwy'n casáu awyrgylch y lle yma, y chwerwedd*' ('I hate the atmosphere of this place, the bitterness'). I'm now living in an atmosphere that's suggested in the second aspect of Isidore of Seville's definition of 'antidote'. The second root, derived from the Greek, suggests treatment,

> by similarity, as indicated by the term πίκρα (i.e. 'remedy, bitter thing'), which is translated as 'bitterness' (amara) because its taste is bitter (amarus). Amara got its name appropriately, because the bitterness (amaritudo) of disease is usually resolved by bitterness.

This 'cure' is just as bad as the poison it's meant to counteract. If Eryl is trying to knock me into shape, this astringent regime is doing more harm than good.

Whenever I try to cut back on activities aside from schoolwork, I come under pressure not to. I tell our minister on several occasions that I don't want to be confirmed in chapel but he bulldozes me into it, asking me what does it profit me if I gain the whole world but lose my soul? My parents persuade me that I'd better do what he says. I hate being in the school's public-speaking team, try to withdraw, but my fellow members persuade me not to. One teacher wants me to go to Oxford to read history. I decide that I like English literature and that I'll apply to Cambridge, which has a more progressive curriculum. He retorts I don't have a cuckoo's chance and begins a bullying campaign so obvious that other teachers complain about it and refer him to the headmaster, who deals with it.

Just before Christmas, a letter arrives informing me that I've been awarded a place at Girton College, Cambridge. We're all delighted. Once the news spreads in school, I have a different problem. One of my favourite teachers, who's spent time teaching me how to write in strict meter Welsh verse, is a fervent nationalist who believes that Welsh students should stay in Wales. She never speaks to me again. I'm getting grief from all sides. Everybody has their own agenda for me. Nobody's listening.

I'm so depressed by now, so worn down by the conflicts at home, that I've stopped keeping the diary. The day of my eighteenth birthday is so wretched that it stands out, leading me to make a now rare entry:

> 18th birthday *gwych – dim un anrheg. Un carden drwy'r post, a 2 garden o'r teulu – Dad heb hyd yn oed weld yr un oddi wrtho fe. 'Roedd e fod i fod yn rywbeth* special – miserable day.
>
> (Excellent 18th birthday – not one present. One card through the post and 2 cards from the family – Dad hadn't even seen the one from him. It was meant to be something special – miserable day.)
>
> (4 November 1977)

When I express my disappointment, I'm reproached for being greedy and unrealistic. The box of After Eight mints that appears at the weekend does nothing to cheer me up. I've come of age and am legally free to vote and marry, but feel more trapped than ever.

The highlight of my year is a school exchange that brings a Breton girl to stay with us. I'm taking French for A level and I love it. A new language, I sense, is a passport to a different body. I'm lucky to be partnered with M, a tiny, very bright girl my age who shows me how to put my long hair up in a chignon. Her skin is flawless and she uses eau de cologne, wears very tight jeans, a brown Breton sweater with buttons on a placket at one shoulder. I imitate her shamelessly. M has been raised speaking Breton, so her relationship with French is like mine with English. We enjoy ourselves together enormously and exchange long letters.

On my first visit to Brittany, I'm thrown in at the linguistic deep end. M's parents are farmers and don't speak a word of English. M's mother is a tiny terror of a woman who sang lustily as she gave birth to her daughter. I once see her chasing after M with a broom but I notice that, unlike me, M isn't afraid of her mother. She laughs at her and does what she wants to anyway.

A new language is a mood-altering drug. My visit to Brittany changes my body and gives me a new personality to inhabit, one that's not ground down by enduring misery at home. I love my new Breton friends. M has a boyfriend, whom I like, and we visit him, drink wine, smoke Gauloises Bleues and talk for hours on end. We go to *festoù noz*, folk music nights on town squares, in which the crowds dance in long, intricate lines, folding back on themselves, like Celtic decorative lettering. I think this a huge improvement on the partner-based Welsh folk dancing, which is bouncy and anti-erotic. I find the small, repetitive movements of linking little fingers with your neighbour, to describe abstract spirals with your hands, while stepping back and forth, with incremental steps to the side, to the commanding bombardes and biniou pipes hypnotic, democratic and joyful.

As ever, I don't want to go home. My diary switches between Welsh and French: '*Cael coffi, commencer à pleurer à la cause de plusieurs choses*' ('Had coffee, started to cry for several reasons') (30 July 1977). To M, I pretend I'm upset about school because I can't confide that I'm dreading life back with my parents. I'm delivered back to Château Despair by a company of twenty Bretons, who've travelled over for a summer trip to Wales. I've come into my own socially and, suddenly, I'm in demand. For example, on the night of 28 September, seven friends phone, two with invitations to go out (one on a date).

I accept an invitation to go to a party. Eryl loses her temper:

> *Row am nos Sul – a ddylswn i fynd. Mae 'ngwerthoedd i mor* confused. *Mam yn cymeryd yn ganiatáol fy mod i'n derbyn rhai pethau, pan fo'n agwedd i wedi newid.* Clash *ofnadwy.*
>
> (Row about Sunday evening – should I go. My values are so confused. Mam taking for granted that I accept certain things, when my attitude has changed. Terrible clash.)
>
> (28 September 1977)

After staying with M, I've had a glimpse of how a more mature family treats their daughter and that has changed me. Eryl senses the shift and hates it.

My final summer at home before going to university is busy. On another trip to Brittany to visit M, I meet B. He's a kind, roly-poly Breton in a brown and cream Icelandic sweater, has a head of long dark hair, a beard and lovely brown eyes. He thinks I'm wonderful and, of course, I'm a sucker for this. My parents are instantly Against.

I know that it isn't sensible to start a new relationship before going off to Cambridge and tell B so, but emotionally, he races ahead of me at a hundred miles an hour. He gives me a ring with Celtic decorations carved into it and the words '*Da Viken*' ('For Ever') in Breton on the inside. I think this is premature. Besides, the ring is a little too tight for my finger, which swells around it. I don't tell him. B invites me to stay with his mother and, in addition, tactlessly suggests that he comes over to drive me up to Cambridge. This is an important ritual for parents who have stood by their child through the ardours of education and exams. Eryl and Gwilym, deeply uneasy, use every argument they can think of to persuade me to finish with B. What they don't know is that he's already proposed marriage, which shocks me. Had Eryl and Gwilym been more restrained in their hostility to B, I could have confided in them but my own pride and stubbornness now prevent me from sharing my unease and the full complexity of the situation with them. As it is, I tell no one anything.

I discover that summer that Eryl is not the only bully in the house. Looking through old letters I kept, I recently found notes that Gwilym had written on the back of National Eisteddfod tickets (the festival was in Cardiff in 1978), coaching me in reasons why I should refuse B's invitation to spend a further two weeks in Brittany before going up to Cambridge:

PRACTICALITIES

1 G. wedi cael gwyliau da yr haf hwn 3 wythnos + wythnos yn Llydaw
Wythnos yn <u>*Glanllyn*</u> *i ddod.*

2 Ychydig wythnosau ar ôl i ddarparu o ran darllen a phethau eraill i Gaergrawnt.

3 Mae ennill ei lle yng Ghaergrawnt wedi golygu llawer o ymdrech ar ran G – ac <u>*eraill,*</u> *mae'n gyfle sy'n dod unwaith mewn bywyd ac yn haeddu ei dderbyn yn ddifrifol.*

Bydd G yn cael ei chymharu â bobl – mor alluog a MWY galluog – o hyn ymlaen a bydd angen mwy o 'application' i gadw i fynd.

Hefyd – (y mae, a) bydd Caergrawnt yn draul ariannol (croeso iddi ei gael – ond iddi gyfiawnhau yr aberth yn y pendraw).

4 All G ddim affordddio pythefnos arall o wyliau i fod ar gael i 'entertaino' y brawd o Lydaw.
– Bydd ysgol wedi ail gychwyn erbyn hynny.

5 Ar wahan i ddarllen etc. bydd galwadau ereill ar amser G. siopa – chwilio – Gwaith tŷ.

———

Felly – byddai'n well i beidio cymhlethu'r sefyllfa mwy ar hyn o bryd. Mae pellter yn obstacl i'r gyfathrach hwn a gwell i dorri'r 1978 gweithgareddau nawr.

Ni welaf fod yn bractical i nhwy'u dau deithio yn ôl ac ymlaen o Gymru i Lydaw – o ran treiliau ariannol.

(PRACTICALITIES

1 G. has had a good holiday this summer 3 weeks + a week in Brittany.
A week in Glanllyn [the Welsh League of Youth's camp in north Wales, where I'd volunteered] to come.

2 Few weeks left to prepare reading and other things for Cambridge.

3 Winning a place in Cambridge has meant a lot of effort on Gwyneth's part – and others, it's an opportunity that comes once in a lifetime and deserves to be accepted seriously.

G will be compared with people – as gifted and MORE gifted – from now on and more 'application' will be required to keep going.

Also – Cambridge is and will be a financial drain (she's welcome to have it – as long as she justifies the sacrifice in the long run.)

4 G can't afford another fortnight of holiday to be on hand to 'entertain' the brother from Brittany.
– School will have recommenced by then.

5 Aside from reading etc. there will be other calls on G's time – shopping – searching – Housework.

———

Therefore – it would be better not to complicate the situation further at the moment. Distance is an obstacle to this intercourse and better to cut the 1978 activities now.

I don't see that it's practical for them both to travel back and forth from Wales to Brittany – in terms of expenses.)

There's a lot of common sense in this prompt sheet. My parents were always extremely generous with helping us with our education, both in terms of time and also financially. This they did without question. The note about school having returned in September is shorthand for Eryl needing to concentrate exclusively on work and not be disturbed by visitors. The 'shopping' and 'housework' reasons seem to me now to be grasping at straws: none of us ever went in much for either. The problem is that B is never named or treated as a person in this sheet. Whatever he is to me, he's simply an obstacle to the Lewis family. There is such a thing as being right in the wrong way.

Gwilym is quick to see a person from outside the family as a threat, and willing to exert pressure on me to get rid of him. When it came to the greatest threat of all to me – Eryl's behaviour – he does nothing. And I needed protection. On 24 August, five weeks before I'm due to go to Cambridge, I record:

> *Gwneud dim byd trwy'r dydd. Row gyda Mam yn y nos – dyw hi methu fy ngodde i. Fe fwrodd hi fi am slammo drws fel 'ma hi wastad yn gwneud.*
>
> (Did nothing all day. Row with Mam in the night – she can't stand me. She hit me for slamming a door like she always does.)
>
> (24 August 1978)

Two days earlier, I'd been allowed to spend a scandalous seven pounds on an international phone call in order to finish with 'the brother from Brittany'. Because my feelings are so ambiguous, I don't succeed. My 'translations' of Gwilym's instructions into French crib notes suggest why this might have been. They're far from being accurate renderings of my parents' desires. I'm very concerned with not wanting to '*induire en erreur*' (mislead) or '*tromper*' (deceive) B. This is my ropey French for 'leading B on'. Here's my summary of what I have to do: '*il faut que je travaille un peu, et respecte ce que mes parents veulent*' ('I must work a bit and respect what my parents want'). Respect was big in our house, but worked only one way. The following statement was, surely, unauthorised: '*On ne peut pas faire l'amour par telephone*' ('One can't make love on the telephone'). We weren't having sex, but it's clearly on our minds. I can now see that the messages that I'm giving B are hopelessly mixed. He could, with good reason, have taken this statement as a signal that I didn't want to finish after all.

The following day, B calls for an hour and a half and I try again to bring things to a conclusion. I've been bullied out of my own point of view so much that I have no idea what I want to happen nor how to enforce it. No matter how often I tell him that he's going too quickly for me, he can't hear that the relationship isn't going to work out. My parents' interference does nothing to clear my head and allows him to say that I'm being pressurised to do what they want. On 25 August, B phones again, and I retreat into French in my diary but confusion reigns:

> *Fe ffoniodd B yn y bore – chwarae teg iddo. Gofyn si c'était la situation ici qui m'a changée ou si c'etait moi qui avait changée?* I responded ~~the latter~~ sorri the former.
>
> (B phoned in the morning – fair play to him. Asked if it was the situation here had changed me or if it was me who'd changed. I responded ~~the latter~~ sorry the former.)
>
> (25 August 1978)

I can't even tell the difference between the former and the latter. Other people's wishes are so loud in my mind that I have no idea what I want and, what's more, no chance of finding out.

I'm missing from my own life.

Chapter 7
CRISIS

A person who's been seriously abused as a child is a house built on a sinkhole. It's only a matter of time before unusually heavy rainfall and gravity sweep away the foundations and your ruined property is uninsurable.

Having seen B off (as they thought), my parents delivered me to Girton College, Cambridge, at the beginning of the 1978 academic year with some colourful pillowcases and a tin full of Welsh cakes. B didn't take the blindest bit of notice of their discouragement and visited anyway a few weeks later. But, as was inevitable, the relationship foundered and eventually we finished. I regret that I wasn't able to be clear with him much sooner. I still find it very difficult to discover what I want and to stick with it because I now automatically experience the extreme remorse that I was forced into by my parents, even though they're long dead. If you're taught that you're not reliable, you end up doubting all your decisions.

Did I have the scent of a victim about me? In my subject group, I soon attract the attention of a female fellow student who dubs me 'the Welsh virgin'. This is technically accurate but not what she means and she mocks my innocence mercilessly. I don't know if this woman is flirting with me or trying to destroy my morale. At an inter-college party in town, my tormentor notices that a certain man is interested in me. Thinking to make me jealous, she pursues him and, one evening, waits for me in the porter's lodge in her dressing gown, displaying a livid choker of love bites around her throat. Triumphant, she informs me who's given them to her then says that she and he had speculated as to whether I'd lose my virginity with a cucumber, which was more obscenity than I've ever heard in my life. Years later, one of my teachers admits that she still feels guilty that the college didn't step in earlier to stop this bizarre campaign. I laugh, telling her that my problems at home were so much more serious that I'd barely registered this strange behaviour. By the end of the term, this troubled person disappeared, after setting a college kitchen on fire and being sent home.

Having finally finished with B, I start going out with my first serious boyfriend. R 'wins' me at a pretend game of cards. At a party, when I go to the bathroom, a friend of his confides that he wants to ask me out. Grabbing some squares of individually wrapped cheese, R shuffles them and proposes that they gamble for me and promptly calls a winning hand. Although he's Welsh, when he and Eryl meet, they recognise each other, correctly, as mortal enemies. I've written about this encounter before, in *Sunbathing in the Rain* and can't better it now. Eryl and R were, in some ways, mirror images of each other:

> My mother and R hated each other on sight. He lit up a cigarette in the house without asking permission and she ended up refusing to speak English whenever he was there. They fought over me like cats. I tried to make them both part of my life but they were oil and water and refused to be mixed. In the end the power struggle became so intense that I felt myself disappear between them.

As we get to know each other better – and see intimately how each other's family works – R is shocked and angry on my behalf about the parental tyranny under which I'm living. I now had company in my fight against my parents' domination of me.

I feel sorry for anybody who falls in love with a damaged person. They have no idea what their fishing nets have caught, what unfamiliar specimen they've hauled up from living under pressures that have distorted their emotions, given them strange backbones, angler lights in order to live at dark depths. They've pulled up a catch that, however desirable, thrashes so violently on the surface that it can swamp the boat and sink it entirely.

My diaries are silent about most of my first year in Cambridge because I'm too busy enjoying the fun I've previously been denied. Having a boyfriend and a group of friends is a full-time occupation, and my daily life is irregular. R is immensely sociable and enjoys being in a group. One night we stay out on the river at Grantchester, light a bonfire and drink till dawn. One of our friends strips to his underpants, dives into the river and is stopped by the police briefly as he jogs, dripping, through the lightening streets of Cambridge. We have to buy a certain number of meals in college each term, but I never seem to be able to organise myself to be present at hall, with its subsidised meals, so a lot of my grant goes on alcohol and meals in Cambridge pubs and restaurants. Attending lectures is beyond me, on the whole. Starting on Consulate, a menthol cigarette, I apply myself to being a smoker, hiding behind the same fug as my father did in his garage at home. I do the bare minimum academically and my report at the end of the year notes, unenthusiastically, that my work was consistent and of an acceptable standard.

There is one exception to this, which I owe to Eryl's talent as a teacher. Mary Ann Radzinowicz – 'Lady Radz' – is one of the most eccentric tutors in college, an American who dresses in long kaftans, chain-smokes through tutorials, which she conducts draped on a chaise longue. She has an acerbic tongue but my understanding of Milton draws high praise from her. When I was in the sixth form, Eryl had been my English teacher. She was brilliant at conveying the imaginative worlds of Chaucer, Jane Austen and in particular Milton. She was known for not having favourites in class, and drew good work from the less academic students without losing the interest of those who, like me, were obsessed with literature. I felt lucky to have her as a teacher, though I was less than thrilled when, one day, when I was sniffing in class, she broke the fourth wall, leant over and handed me a tissue. She marked me harder than the rest of the class. I can't wait to convey this Cambridge triumph of hers in a letter to Eryl:

> *Annwyl Pawb,*
>
> *Wel – dyma syndod. Ail lythyr mewn wythnos! Peidiwch poeni, 'does dim byd gwael wedi digwydd. Dim on 'sgwennu 'yf fi i ddweud peth newyddion diddorol.*
>
> *MAM – mi fyddwch yn* thrilled *gan hyn! Mae Lady Ratzinovitz [sic] yn danfon ei llongyfarchiadau atoch am fod yn athrawes mor dda, ac am gael barn dda am Milton. A mae hi'n awdurdod! Mi ddarllennais i fy nghraethawd allan ar Milton's* grand style *– (un wedi ei seilio ar yr un wnes i i chi yn yr ysgol) ac fe ddwedodd hi ar y diwedd bod angen fy llongyfarch i am draethawd da iawn. Wedyn (ar ôl gwydriad o* sherry*) fe ddilynnodd y sgwrs ganlynol (mi sgwennes i e lawr yn syth, er mwyn ei gofio'n union i chi –*
>
> Lady R: Who taught you Milton, Miss Lewis?
>
> Gwyn: My mother.
>
> Lady R: Well ..[.] Not only is she to be congratulated on being a very effective teacher, but, also, in my view for being RIGHT about Milton!
>
> *Wel, wel, wel, Mrs. Lewis! ...*
>
> *Dim ond meddwl o'n i y byddech chi'n lico gwybod beth ddigwyddodd heddi – llongyfarchiadau, Mam.*

> (Dear Everybody,
>
> Well – here's a surprise. A second letter in a week! Don't worry, nothing bad has happened. I'm only writing to tell you some interesting news.
>
> MAM – you'll be thrilled by this! Lady Ratzinovitz [*sic*] sends her congratulations to you for being such a good teacher, and for having a good opinion of Milton. And she's an authority! I read out my essay on

> Milton's grand style – (one based on the one I did for you in school) and she said at the end that I should be congratulated for a very good essay. Then (after a glass of sherry) the following conversation followed
>
> (I wrote it down straight away, in order to remember it exactly for you –
>
> Lady R: Who taught you Milton, Miss Lewis?
>
> Gwyn: My mother.
>
> Lady R: Well ..[.] Not only is she to be congratulated on being a very effective teacher, but, also, in my view for being RIGHT about Milton!
>
> Well, well, well, Mrs. Lewis! ...
>
> I only thought that you would like to know what happened today – congratulations, Mam.
>
> (postmarked 13 January 1979)

For once, it's good to be able to build Eryl's self-esteem, which was in short supply. I wonder also if I feared that, without her guidance, I was not going to be able to hold my own academically. This is the double-edged sword of being dominated as a child. You're desperate to break free but you've also been taught that you're so useless that you need the person who's terrorising you.

By the summer of 1979, although I adore R, I'm bored by always being in company. I've abdicated my thinking to my boyfriend, given too much of myself away. I feel that I'd lost contact with the internal voice to which I'd made my childhood vow. My decision to down tools as a poet in response to Eryl's co-option of my work is now hurting me more than it is her. I need to reclaim interior territory for myself and to jolt my brain into action again with a period of reading and solitude. I want to find out what I'm capable of intellectually and creatively.

R and I are both fiery characters with ample reserves of wilfulness and we row with growing frequency. R often objects to something I've done – whether I'm in the wrong (I often am) or not – I have to beg forgiveness before he comes round. R can't understand why I'm so submissive to my parents' wishes and he accuses me of lacking integrity and the courage to stand up to them. We go to Canterbury for the weekend but I'm so anxious that Eryl and Gwilym will find out (I know that they'll disapprove) that I can't relax and enjoy the trip. I know this isn't normal but my body's still living in Château Despair. The summer at the end of our first year in Cambridge, he goes off to Ireland alone to think about whether our relationship has a future or if I'm to be placed in the next drawer down from a rejected God. On the other hand, Eryl tells me that, if R and I ever go to live with each other, it will kill her.

Where do you go when life at home is a bed of nettles and your boyfriend, whom you love fiercely, has gone? My college allows students to rent rooms during the summer holidays. I leap at the chance.

My room that summer was at the top of the redbrick tower which stands over the entrance to the Girton porter's lodge. Girton was founded in 1869 and was the first Cambridge college for women. The building was designed by Alfred Waterhouse in the same inflamed redbrick Gothic style as London's Natural History Museum. With my hyper-acute hearing, I'm always trying to get away from everybody else because I find the sound of music and conversation insanely distracting. A narrow arch on the top floor of the college hides a tiny spiral staircase that leads up a further three flights to the top of the tower, where the flagpole stood and from whose redbrick mock-crenelations you can lean out and see miles of flat Cambridgeshire land. Tower 4 is immediately under this viewpoint. It's impractical because the room has no running water so, in order to make tea, wash dishes or use the bathroom, I've to scurry up and down two flights of a spiral staircase barely wide enough for one person but I don't care.

The room is glorious. It has sash windows on two sides – though my memory insists on adding a third that isn't there. I keep everything open for the cross-breeze. One afternoon, I watch a thunderstorm approach the college from miles away. I open all the windows and let it go through me and the room, curtains billowing and papers flying everywhere. I'm away from people and in the jet-stream, exactly where I want to be.

Stafell awelon a golau'r haul ... Dyma'r tro cyntaf i fi fod yn wirioneddol ar fy mhen fy hun ers i mi fynd i America.

(Room of breezes and sunlight ... This is the first time I've truly been on my own since I went to America.)
(12 July 1979)

Rapunzel has put herself in her tower and pulled up the rope ladder.

Suspended, for a few precious weeks, above the emotional terrain in which I'd been brought up, I see clearly what's happening. In a good sign for my mental health, I'm keeping a diary again in an old school notebook covered in wrapping paper with an Italian Renaissance pattern.

I tell myself my own story in the past tense. I have no intention of making it my future:

Ofnai ei mham – ymddangosai llid y wraig yn hollol gyfiawn, yn gyflawn ac yn ordeiniedig (cyn iddi fedru barnu resymoldeb). Dyma oedd natur dicter Duw – nid i'w ddeall, ond i ymateb iddo mewn defosiwn ac ysbryd edifar ... Gofynnodd un iddi ei briodi. Gadawodd ef, ond 'roedd ei gariad, fel y glaw, wedi pery blodeuo ynddi.

Daeth i Gaergrawnt, bron ar ddamwain. Driftodd yn emosiynnol yn ei blwyddyn gyntaf heb wybod beth yr oedd ganddi hawl i'w gymeryd oddi wrth y lle. A llithrodd i gariad. Beth nesaf?

Dechreuodd sylweddoli na fedrai fyw ei bywyd yn ôl syniadau pobl eraill. Neu, o leiaf, ganddi hi yr oedd yr hawl i ddewis pa seren a ddylynai [sic].

Daeth yn frwydr rhwng hen ffyddlondeb a llwon newydd, rhai a ymgymerodd, nid oherwydd arfer na'r ymlyniant a ddisgwylid ganddi, ond oherwydd greddf, a dewis na fedrai egluro. Rheidrwydd rhyfeddol – ond poenus. Ni ddaw gwreiddiau hen goeden ond yn styfnig o gynhesrwydd y pridd.

(She feared her mother – the woman's rage appeared totally justified, complete and ordained (before she was able to judge reasonableness). This was the nature of God's wrath – not to be understood, but to be responded to with devotion and a repentant spirit … One asked her to marry him. She left him but his love, like the rain, caused a blossoming in her

She came to Cambridge almost by accident. She drifted emotionally in her first year without knowing what she had the right to take from the place. And slipped into love. What next?

She began to realise that she couldn't live her life according to other people's ideas. Or, at least, that it was she who had the right to choose which star she followed.

It came to a fight between an old faithfulness and new vows, which she undertook, not because of habit or an adherence that was expected of her, but because of instinct, and a choice that she couldn't explain. A wondrous necessity – but painful. The roots of an old tree only come stubbornly from the soil's warmth.)

(20 July 1979)

My analysis of the situation is robust but also takes into account Eryl's difficulties at school:

Am bod bywyd Mam allan o reolaeth (gorfod dysgu, casineb yn yr ysgol) gwna ei gorau i'n cadw o fewn 4 mur ei thŷ. Yno, ei hwyliau hi yw'r haul, a'i thymer hi sydd â'r nerth i wneud pawb yn hapus neu yn ddiflas. Dyma'r unig amgylchfyd lle hi yw'r frenhines. A dyma pam na hoffa adael y tŷ i fynd ar wyliau, gan fod yn rhaid iddi blygu eto i reolau cwrteisi ac ymddygiad deche eto.

(Because Mam's life is out of control (having to teach, malice in school), she does her best to keep us inside the 4 walls of her house. There, her moods are the sun, and it's her temper that has the strength to make everybody happy or miserable. This is the only environment in which she is the queen. And this is why she doesn't like leaving the house to go on holiday, because she has to bend again to the rules of courtesy and decent behaviour again.)

(30 July 1979)

My real goal in Cambridge that summer is to start writing. This is far from easy after a period of willed silence:

Mae hi mor hawdd ildio eich ymatebion yn llwyr i ffordd rhn. arall o weld y byd. Mae'n fwy anodd gorfod torri sianel eich bywyd eich hun. Ond, mi dreia i wneud hynny – os parha i fis! Rhaid i fi gael fy hunan yn strêt, rhoi trefn ar bopeth.

(It's so easy to yield your reactions completely to how sbdy. else sees the world. It's harder to cut the channel of your own life. But I'll try to do that – if I last a month! Must get myself straight, put everything in order.)

(14 July 1979)

I suspect that I'm wanting to distance myself from domination by R as much as my parents, even though I'm in love with him. The relief of being away from rows at home soon gives way, though, in my tower, to a devastating loneliness. The only other student I meet in college is a girl who also has problems at home. Neither of us elaborates. One evening, I cycle into town and sit, eating fish and chips on a wall near Jesus College, watching groups of tourists and feeling desolate:

Peth ofnadwy yw bod mewn tref heb gartref, ac edrych o'r tu allan ar gysur a sicrwydd pobl eraill, heb unman tebyg eich hun.

(It's a terrible thing to be in a town without a home, looking from the outside at other people's comfort and security, without anywhere similar yourself.)

(21 July 1979)

In town, I watch the poet and don J. H. Prynne looking like '*gweinidog Methodist seimllyd*' ('a greasy Methodist minister') carefully search inside two brown paper bags, tear each one in half and, with great care, deposit them in a litter bin. I describe the qualities of my ideal future home:

Mi welaf dŷ, ond nid oes eto furiau iddo. Ni wn ai mewn pant ai ar ben allt, mewn pentref neu mewn dinas y bydd. Ond yno, mi obeithiaf bydd y drws ar agor i'r awyr oriog, yr heulwen a'r glaw. Ni fydd ystafelloedd yn grothau o farwolaeth, celloedd o ddihangfa, cysgodion ac ofn. Bydd arswyd yno, bydd – ond fe'i gwelir ar ford y gegin, a bydd yn fellt yn yr awyr – gobeithio. Bydd y drws ar agor, a bydd pryd a gwely i bawb a ddaw. Stafelloedd blodau, a golau a chariad.

(I see a house but it doesn't yet have walls. I don't know if it will be in a dip or on top of a hill, in a village or in a city. But there, I hope that the door will be open to the changeable air, the sunshine and the rain. The rooms won't be wombs of death, cells of escape, shadows and fear. There will be terror there, yes – but it will be seen on the kitchen table, and it will be lightning in the air – I hope. The door will be open, and there will be a meal and a bed for everybody who comes. Rooms of flowers, and light and love.)

(18 July 1979)

I would have been surprised, then, to learn that I'm writing this now from the same house that I wanted to escape. Same architecture, no flowers, but the atmosphere could not be more different. There are no curtains on the windows, so the light streams in. There's nothing that can't be said between me and Leighton. We live in a married abundance.

This isn't competition writing, but a fight for my own life:

> *Breuddwydio neithiwr fy mod i mewn gardd gyda Dad a Mam, a tŷ tywyll y tu ôl i ni. Torrai llwybr trwy ddiffaethwch yr ardd, fel cyllell yn agor llysieuyn. 'Roedd y mieri mawr, danheddog yn glymau ffyrnig o'n cylch. Gwreiddiau blewog, tew yn cordeddi yn wenwynog ar hyd y tir, gan guddio'r goleuni a phob glendid. Teimlwn anobaith wrth edrych ar y clymau – ni fedrwn i â chrib tila fy rheswm eu datod.*
>
> (Dreamt last night that I was in a garden with Dad and Mam, and a dark house behind us. A path cut through the garden's jungle, like a knife cutting a vegetable. The large, toothed brambles were fierce knots around us. Hairy, fat roots twisted, poisonous, across the soil, hiding the light and all beauty. I felt despair looking at the knots – I couldn't untangle them with the puny comb of my reason.)
>
> (18 July 1979)

My subconscious explains what's going on with admirable clarity. Decades later, I'm still disentangling myself from these toxic roots.

The respite in my Cambridge tower is temporary. Two days after this entry, I climb up to my room after being in town, only to find that a storm cloud has taken up residence on one of the walls. The harvest has disturbed the insects hiding in the crops and a swarm of thunder bugs, or thrips, has taken flight, found the windows of my room open and taken up residence. I study an individual on the back of my hand. It's tiny, like a rebellious punctuation mark, ending with a sharp upswept tail, a comma. I can't decide if the itch in my skin is psychosomatic or if thrips actually sting. They do. Bugs cover my desk, they're in the pages of my books, like tiny psychopathic writing. I stay in the room as long as I can, then go for help.

My parents come to visit for the weekend, which gives me hope that they will begin to see me as an adult: '*Am y tro cynta, 'rwy'n teimlo yn annibynnol, fel pe baent yn ymwelwyr, ac nid yn* visiting angels of retribution!!'('For the first time, I feel independent, as if they were visitors, and not visiting angels of retribution!!') (20 July 1979). A few days later, the boyfriend writes to say that he loves me after all and that we are still on. I flee the Tower and catch the train to Cardiff for a blissful reunion. We slip up the valleys to stay with R's hospitable and tolerant parents without letting mine know that I'm back. However, those weeks of thinking, painful as they are, have changed me and this places a wall between us.

When I return to my parents in Cardiff, despite my hopes, nothing has changed. In a furious row, Eryl says that, had I gone home instead of visiting R, I would have saved them a trip to Cambridge. '*Sgrech fewnol*' ('internal scream'), I comment. She then accuses me of:

> *troi fy nghefn ar bethau Cymreig, gadael cyllyll yn y gyp room, gwisgo'n* scruffy … *Ai fi sy'n wallgo i feddwl nad oes pwysigrwydd i'r pethau hyn? Fy noson gyntaf adre ar ôl 3 wythnos, ac fe'm erlidir fel plentyn am adael fy meic y tu allan i'r coleg.*
>
> (turning my back on Welsh things, leaving knives in the gyp room [kitchen], dressing scruffily … Am I mad to think that these things aren't important? My first night home after 3 weeks and I'm persecuted like a child for leaving my bike outside the college.)
>
> (23 July 1979)

Even though I've been away from home for a year and stay regularly with R's family about forty minutes away from Cardiff, that summer Eryl insists – she the atheist – that I be home for

Sunday lunch every week, as if it were holy. Having forced me, by emotional blackmail, to return, she then ignores me. The meal is eaten in near silence then, having proved her power to compel me home, Eryl and Gwilym would go to sleep for the rest of the afternoon. I'm left to creep around the house – woe betide anybody who wakes the sleepers! – enraged and despising myself for being a pushover.

Eryl should have been much more concerned about the knives that have appeared in my notebook. There's no need for a qualification as a psychoanalyst to parse this frank dream, the unconscious is painted in bold strokes:

> *Breuddwydio fy mod i'n anweledig, ac yn cael fy erlid gan frenhines baganaidd yn brandisho cyllyll erchrydus. 'Roeddwn i mewn pydew – stafell mewn tŷ gweledig, a'r wraig yma'n ceisio fy ffeindio trwy dwyll, gan fy mod wedi rhedeg mor gyflym ar hyd y meysydd. Fe ollyngodd wyau o'r tô er mwyn gweld os amharai fy nghorff eu cwymp. Mi a'u hosgoiais. Yna, gwrando am fy anadl. A minnau yma yn fy ngwely yn gwrando hefyd ac yn arswydo wrth glywed fy anadlu!*
>
> (Dream I'm invisible, and being pursued by a pagan queen brandishing dreadful knives. I was in a well – a room in a visible house, and this woman trying to find me by trickery, as I'd run so fast across the fields. She dropped eggs from the roof, in order to see if my body impeded their fall. I avoided them. Then, listened for my breath. And me here in my bed listening too and being horrified as I hear my breathing!)
>
> (19 July 1979)

I know that if I give myself away, I'm going to be stabbed. The emotional truth of how I'm living is that every breath makes me a target. Reading it back makes me want to hyperventilate. I don't have to do anything wrong. I *am* wrong.

An even more dangerous knife is already inside my brain. Struggling to express my desperation in words, I've begun to draw images of my situation. The art is childish but expressive. On the first of August, I portray myself with a massive blade over the left side of my face. The knife depicts Eryl's assault on me and is shaded with angry zigzag hatching, as if molecules are oscillating inside the steel. Like a Venn diagram, I've drawn in a deeper patch of dark which is the overlap between the blade and my cheek. I've noted in a bubble above: '*Dyma lle y dylset ti fod yn claddu*' ('This is where you should be digging'). Above the left eyebrow is a slim sword – used in the tarot minor arcana cards to represent reason – which I now read as a determination to use my intellect to fight the emotional violence being done to me.

Knife drawing from the diary

With my experience now of decades of migraine, I'm fascinated to notice that the two blades are laid across the parts of the trigeminal nerve that hurt me the most during an attack. Over forty years on, I'm living the echoes of this earlier anguish in my nerves. Physical and emotional pain converse with each other over many years. My brain is migrainous today and is having difficulty looking at what happens next to my younger self. I'm also nauseous. This tale is poisoning me again.

—Don't give up now, Gwyn, this will inoculate you in the future. This is only pain. Joy comes in the morning.

Later in the summer of 1979, the nightmares I've described move out of my dreams and form a real-life phantasmagoria. I'm staying with my boyfriend's family and, faced with the usual prospect of having to go home for the punitive Sunday lunch, I feel that there's a large spider sitting over my face. Nearly hysterical, I whisper this to my boyfriend, who becomes very concerned. Not only am I hallucinating, I'm running a temperature. I phone home to say that I'm not well and so will be staying put for a few days. This is serious rebellion. I'm feverish and know that, if I give in, I'll go insane.

Eryl insists that, if I'm ill, I have to come home, ignoring the fact that home is what has made me so sick. There's shouting and screaming and the phone is thrust into my father's hands:

'You talk to her, Gwilym.'

So he comes on, all reasonable tone of voice, but it's violent, nevertheless, enforcing the iron message:

'Come home. You have to come home.'

I'm accused of showing up my parents, of imposing on my boyfriend's family, of being, as usual, selfish. Decades after this assault, thinking about it makes my left eye throb. Both parents thrust the knife through my eye, deep into my brain. Listen to sense, they hiss, come home. The phone call goes on and on, as the emotional blackmail continues. If I slip from the grip of one argument, they try another and hold tighter.

'Here, speak to your sister!'

Hostage as she is herself, Marian tries to say something that won't make things worse for her. I'm sobbing and nobody'll leave me alone to curl up and sleep. We reach an impasse and I end the call. They phone back and wear me down, ill as I am, by brute force:

'Your father will come to pick you up.'

Having heard only my side of the conversation, the boyfriend goes to the downstairs loo and throws up. I'm still grateful for this honest visceral reaction, it's a benchmark. R's mother, who's been listening to the torture without interfering, which must have taken great restraint, rushes in with a green and gold decanter and posh delicate glasses:

'Give Gwyneth some sherry!'

I gather, years later, from Eryl that she said a few choice words to my mother, which means a lot to me now, but I never learn what she said.

On the way home, Gwilym stops the car in a layby and weeps. He has joined me in what I call '*pydew hunllefau*' ('the well of nightmares').

Soon, after, I'm diagnosed with glandular fever (infectious mononucleosis), which is caused by the Epstein-Barr virus. Nobody else I come into contact with that summer seems to have caught it, so I'm baffled as to where I caught 'the kissing disease'. I now learn that the virus, perhaps acquired in childhood, can lie dormant until a stressed immune system permits it to become active. Research shows that there's 'an association between latent herpesvirus reactivation and attachment anxiety', which I have in spades,[11] so there's a connection between my childhood unhappiness and this infection that has taken advantage of an emotional crisis.

I can no longer keep my distress under control. Both mind and body are unravelling. My diary reflects this emotional and visual disturbance. Illness and emotional damage mean that life can no

---

11 Christopher Fagundes et al., 'Attachment anxiety is related to Epstein–Barr virus latency', *Brain, Behaviour, and Immunity*, 41 (October 2014), 232–8, www.ncbi.nlm.nih.gov/pmc/articles/PMC4304069/?ref=

longer be described in straight lines. The writing breaks up into wavy patterns on the page. These snatches are physically and emotionally difficult to read. My point of view has been blotted out so thoroughly that I pretend that I'm writing in the present, as in a normal diary entry. In a daring imaginative leap, I find the only member of the family that I trust and address is '*Gwyneth y dyfodol, bod nad wyf yn ei hadnabod*' ('The future Gwyneth, a being I don't know').

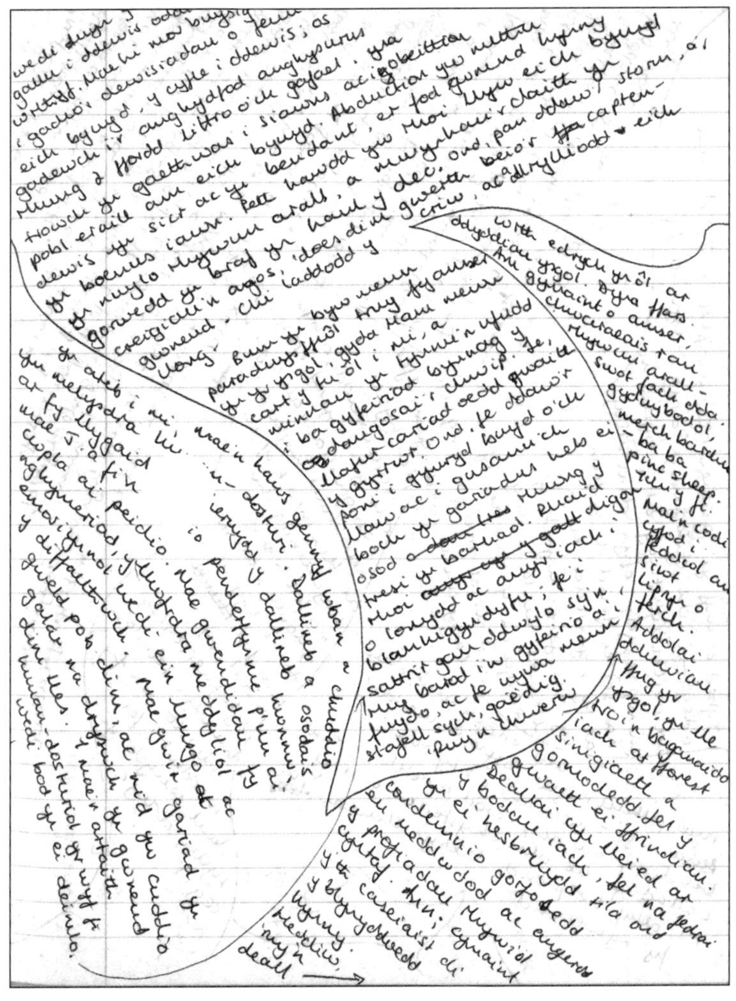

Diary page

This 1979 diary is my first attempt to describe the full truth of what was happening to me, rather than hiding from or covering for my parents. I'm attempting to understand the impossible situation in which I find myself and to outline what I'd like my own mind to be. Most of the writing is cringe-worthy (for its strength of feeling) and excruciatingly bad (which is due to the struggle for sincerity). As I transcribe these diary entries from when I was nineteen, I have the uncanny sense of being two women, each watching the other. There are forty years between us but it's comforting to find that we're both equally committed to finding what we mean and meaning what we say.

This is the bedrock of writing and precedes any exercise of craft. I now have decades of writing poetry behind me and have learned that form brings its own psychological protection. This diary, with its new, raw honesty, is 'writing before form'. These free-floating insights are volatile and, like petrol fumes, can ignite before you're ready and blow up in your face. Soon, I will pay a high price physically and mentally for them. My refusal to write poems any more has robbed me of the safety of aesthetic structure. Words come from the subconscious, crackling with static but don't hit the ground to discharge their electricity. Like ball lightning, that mysterious electrical phenomenon that moves through windows, these insights can burn. They need embodiment in a safe medium – a poem will do it – to make toxic material bearable. Artistic gifts, practised without the discipline which producing an actual work of art demands (humility, persistence in the face of failure, admiration of other artists' productions and the chastening gap between a work as it's imagined and how it turns out), are a dangerous force. Such energy, when it's not safely contained by form, is like a box of fireworks that has caught fire. There's no knowing who'll be hurt.

Nevertheless, the relationship between me now and this shaky Gwyneth, besieged in her tower, is a bridge in time, a foothold that helps us both. Because I'm now giving her my full attention in this book, I'm proof that she does have a friendly witness to her pain and, more importantly, that, together, we've become the writer that she fears she won't be able to be. In turn, young

Gwyneth has shattered my denial about my past. Her honesty then holds me to account now.

In these diary pages, I'm throwing material that I can't handle in the 1980s forward to myself as a future reader – and writer – who can, I hope, deal with it. The younger Gwyneth turns to her older self, even as the younger is making notes for her elder. The 'us' refers to me and R:

> *Cyfnod hesb fu'r haf yma i mi, ac i ninnau. Cyfnod o nerfusrwydd agos i wallgofrwydd o dan pwysau na ddeallwn.*
>
> (This summer has been a barren period for me and for us. A period of nervousness close to madness under pressure that I didn't understand.)

I've been so thoroughly brainwashed that, even now, I believe that my parents are acting out of concern.

> *Mae codi byrdwn fy nghyfrifoldebau fy hun mor anodd i mi. Mae cario'r fath bwysau yn anodd am y tro cyntaf, yn enwedig pan fo ceraint ar bob llaw yn barod i helpu.*
>
> (Lifting the burden of my own responsibilities is so hard for me. Carrying such weight is hard for the first time, especially when loved ones all round are ready to help.)

But reality seeps through:

> *– trwy fy amser yn yr ysgol, gyda Mam mewn cart y tu ôl i mi, a minnau yn tynnu'n ufudd, i ba gyfeiriad bynnag y dangosai'r chwip … [Gartref mae] caledi, creulondeb a dagrau … Drysau pob stafell wedi eu cloi, letis wedi ei olchi'n lân, a dillad wedi eu crasu tan eu bod fel cerrig o sych.*

> (– through my time in school, with Mam in a cart behind me, and me pulling obediently in whichever direction the whip showed me … [Home is] hardship, cruelty and tears … All the doors locked, lettuce washed clean, and clothes aired until they're dry like stones.)

My only hope is '*y bydd gennyf i'r cryfder i wrthryfela yn erbyn melltith Mamgu*' ('that I have the strength to rebel against the curse of Mamgu').

There are three people on top of me, each blaming me for doing the wrong thing in relation to the other. I blame myself for '*gwendidau fy nghymeriad, y llwfrdra meddyliol ac emosiynnol*' ('my character weaknesses, the mental and emotional cowardice') for spoiling the relationship.

—*You were never a coward.*

A few weeks later, my unhappiness has, understandably, driven R to despair and, unable to see a way forward, we finish.

I return to Girton for my second year, still weak from glandular fever, but relieved not to be home, at least for a while. The Christmas of my second year at Cambridge had been unbearable at home. I have no record of why, exactly, but even by our standards, the conflict was intense. Back at college, I can no longer function. A few weeks later and I'm in Girton's sick bay, having had a nervous breakdown. I'm skeletally thin. Around me, panic attacks roll in like thunderstorms that stop me breathing, and make me want to scream in terror. I want out. I haven't attempted suicide, but I'm not far from that point. If things don't change, I'm going to die. Luckily for me, R and I had got back together and he was a faithful and steady support to me throughout this crisis.

I write to my parents explaining that I can't carry on as we are, that I can't take the pressure under which they've put me, and that

I'm in terrible trouble and mentally unwell. If I could, I'd quote this letter but my parents must have destroyed it, though I kept theirs to me. I know that by reproducing the bulk of these letters here, I'm committing an act of gross disloyalty to my parents, even though they're dead. But this interchange is so important in this long process of disentangling myself from them that I hope that you won't think too badly of me. Proof is all. These texts were highly deliberate; they would have been revised and copied out fair. They're touchstones for how my parents saw themselves and me, so I hold them now to account for these words.

The first response comes from my father:

> *Dydd Iau 31 Ionawr/ 80*
>
> *Annwyl Gwyneth Fach,*
>
> *Ychydig o eiriau dros dro. 'Rwyt ti wedi gweled fy nagrau – a 'd oes gennyf ddim cywilydd am hynny – ac y maent yn agos eto o feddwl am beth 'r wyt wedi dioddef – ac mor ifanc. Felly mae rhyw syniad gennyf o'th gyflwr ac o'r cyflwr mae Mam wedi bod ynddo sawl gwaith.*
>
> *Codiad calon oedd gweled dy fod yn ddigon câll i edrych am help yn y llefydd iawn a'i ffindio ac elwa arno. Hefyd i glywed dy fod wedi codi dy hun tipyn ac yn teimlo fel cario ymlaen.*
>
> *Daeth dy lythyr hanner dydd 'ddoe ond 'r wyf heb ei ddangos i Mam eto – mae'n dechrau cyfaddawdu a'i sefyllfa yn Rhydfelen ac mae Marian a minnau yn ei gweld yn berson gwahannol – ond yn cael pyliau o'r iselder weithiau. Yn fwy na thebyg caiff weled y llythyr heno ar ôl te – a disgwyliaf y gei lythyr dros y benwythnos [sic].*
>
> *'Dyw [sic] ddim yn bwriadu dweud am fy llythyr ar hyn o bryd. Efallai gwnaf.*
>
> *Bwriadaf cynghori dy fod yn cael dy adael i ffindio dy ffordd dy hun (nid yn yr ystyr o ddiarddeliad) –*

gobeithio, fel canlyniad o ymgynghori a'r teulu; ac os bydd anghytundeb – boed iddo fod anghytundeb caredig.

Paid ag anobeithio.

'Rwy'n gweddïo drosot – a'r gweddill ohonom

Cariad,

Dad.

(Thursday 31 January/ 80

Dear Little Gwyneth,

A few words for now. You've seen my tears – and I'm not ashamed of that – and they're close again when I think of what you've suffered – and so young. So I have some idea of the state you're in and the state that Mam's been in several times.)

—Notice how he's already talking about Eryl's suffering? This should, for once, be all about you.

(It cheered me up to see that you were sensible enough to look for help in the right places and to find it and profit from it. Also to hear that you've lifted yourself a bit and are feeling like carrying on.

Your letter arrived at noon yesterday but I haven't shown it to Mam yet – she's beginning to reconcile herself to the situation in Rhydfelen [she had switched schools] and Marian and I think she's a different person – but having bouts of depression sometimes. More than likely she can see the letter after tea this evening – and I expect that you'll get a letter over the weekend.

At the moment, I don't intend to say about my letter. Perhaps I will.)

Gwilym's just heard that his daughter's seriously unwell and he keeps the news to himself. I still find it difficult to believe that he did this.

> (I intend to advise that you're allowed to find your own way (not in the sense of being disinherited) – I hope, as a result of consulting with the family; and if there is disagreement, let that be a kind disagreement.)

—He wants you to 'consult' with the family that's killing you.

All the same, I appreciate Gwilym's warm tone and heartfelt encouragement:

> (Don't despair.
> I'm praying for you – and the rest of us.
> Love,
> Dad.)

At the time, I thought his letter kind. But it's not how I read it now. Behind the moderate words is a message. It's such a betrayal that my sight breaks up, but see it I must: You may be in mortal danger but 'the rest of us' together and Eryl, in particular, come first.

Six days after my letter had arrived in Cardiff, a reply came from Eryl. If my daughter had written to say that she was having a breakdown and my husband had kept the fact from me for two seconds, let alone a whole day, I'd have been beside myself. In some ways, Eryl 'gets' the urgency of the situation much fully than Gwilym does:

> *Fel rwy'n siwr rwyt ti'n sylweddoli, roedd dy lythr yn sioc ofnadwy i ni gyd. Fedrwn i ddim wynebu'r ysgol ar ddydd Gwener ar ol ei gael; byddwn wedi hoffi dod lan yn syth, ond roeddem yn parchu beth ddywedes ti dy fod am gael llonydd yn awr nes dy fod wedi dod yn ol at dy hunan yn fwy.*

> (As I'm sure you realise, your letter was a terrible shock to us all. I couldn't face school on Friday after receiving it; I would have liked to have come up straight away, but we respected what you said that you wanted to be left alone now until you've come to yourself more.)

I want to be generous in my response to Eryl's letter. It must have cost her to write because, in it, she admits to her own faults in a way she'd never done before. I read it as an honest attempt to hold herself to account.

> *Mae'r tri ohonom wedi trin a thrafod llawer, ac yn gytun mae'r peth i wneud nawr yw gweld ble aethom yn 'wrong' a cheisio rhoi pethe yn eu lle. Efallai hefyd bod rhai pethe y ddylwn i egluro i ti y bydde'n help i ti ddeall pam rwy i fel yr wyf. Roedd Dad am i mi sgwennu llythr fel hwn i ti yn syth ar ol i ti fynd nol ond rown i'n ffeindio'n anodd gwneud hynny.*

> (The three of us have talked and discussed a lot and we're agreed that the thing to do now is to see where we went 'wrong' and try to put things in their place. Perhaps there are some things I should explain to you that would help you to understand why I am as I am. Dad wanted me to write a letter like this to you straight after you went back but I found it hard to do that.)

It's news to me that Gwilym realised how disastrous the previous Christmas had been for me, but Eryl had refused to put it right.

Eryl continues: '*Efallai bod y ddwy ohom yn rhy debyg*' ('Perhaps the two of us are too alike'). No. I checked with Megan, we're nothing alike. A narcissist sees herself in me. Quelle surprise. The letter goes on:

> *Efallai bod y ddwy ohom yn rhy debyg ac oherwydd hynny fy mod wedi tueddi dy wthio i gyflawni'r pethe y*

byddwn i wedi hoffi'i wneud – llenydda etc. Mae mwy o dalent gennyt ti na fi a hefyd rwyt ti'n meddu ar rywbeth na sydd gen i sef y ddawn o ddod ymlaen gyda phobol yn rhwydd. Fy nghamgymeriad i oedd dy wthio di at lyfrau etc. gan mai yn y cyfeiriad hynny roeddwn i'n cael mwyaf o fwynhad, yn lle dy adael i ddilyn dy natur dy hunan.

(Perhaps the two of us are too alike and because of that I have tended to push you to achieve those things that I would like to have done – writing etc. You have more talent than I do and also you possess something that I don't have, that is, the ability to get along easily with people. My mistake was to push you towards books etc. because that was the direction in which I had most enjoyment, rather than leaving you to follow your own nature.)

Eryl's mistake wasn't misdirecting me towards books at all, it was in her refusal to tolerate any disobedience to her will. But this degree of self-reflection is new and, reading it in my sickbay bed, I'm deeply encouraged by its attempt to put things right.

Efallai y dylwn egluro i ti pam rwy mor 'od', er mwyn i ti gael gweld bod angen help arna i. Mae Dad wedi bod yn gymorth aruthrol i mi drwy'n bywyd priodasol – rwy'n siwr y byddwn wedi mynd 'off *y* rails' *onibai amdano ef gan ei fod yn fwy* 'stable'.

(Perhaps I should explain to you why I'm so 'od', so you can see that I need help. Dad has been a tremendous help to me throughout our married life – I'm sure that I would have gone 'off the rails' if it hadn't been for him because he's more 'stable'.)

I've seen Gwilym calm Eryl down so often that I know that this is true. There were periods in the previous year when I know he's gone to work unsure of what he'd find when he came home. He hid the bleach from under the kitchen sink and, with dread, we'd all think of Whitchurch Mental Hospital. I'd already told Eryl once that she needed psychiatric help, and she never forgave me for suggesting it.

> *Mae'r elfen hon o* 'instability'*, efallai, yn dod o ochr Mamgu [...] Roedd Mamgu yn anodd iawn i fyw gyda hi – doedd yr awyrgylch gartre ddim yn dda. Wrth sortio pethe mas yn Llanddewi ar ôl i Dadcu farw, darganfu Dad a mi mai mater o raid oedd eu priodas. Roedd Mamgu yn sur iawn ac rwy'n siwr bod Dadcu wedi gorfod 'talu' am weddill ei oes.*
>
> (This element of 'instability', perhaps, comes from Mamgu's side ... Mamgu was very difficult to live with – the atmosphere at home wasn't good. As we sorted things out in Llanddewi after Dadcu died, me and Dad discovered that their getting married was a matter of necessity. This was a shock, but it explained a great deal about their relationship. Mamgu was very sour and I'm sure that Dadcu had to 'pay' for the rest of his life.)

When I first read this letter, this is where I cry, out of sadness for my lovely Dacu and for the horrible situation Eryl was brought up in. My heart is harder now and I think that this is a long, long letter about Eryl. Again.

> *Felly ges i ddim o'm magu mewn awyrgylch* 'communicative' *ond mewn awyrgylch o* 'mistrust'*. Roedd Dadcu yn boddi'i hunan yn ei waith yn yr ysgol ac yn gymdeithasol. Mae'r ffaith bod deg mlynedd rhwng Megan a fi yn bwysig hefyd – Megan oedd yn cael ei chanmol o hyd – wedi gwneud yn dda yn academaidd, yn ferch bert, yn gyfeillgar.*

(So I wasn't raised in a 'communicative' atmosphere but in an atmosphere of 'mistrust'. Dadcu drowned himself in his school work and socially. The fact that there are ten years between Megan and me is important too – Megan was the one who was always praised – did well academically, a pretty girl, friendly.)

—*You were right, she's confused you with Megan.*

Up until now I've believed the letter.

Roeddwn i'n cael y teimlad o hyd mai dim ond am fy llwyddiant yn fy ngwaith roeddwn i'n cael fy mharchu – mae hwn mor debyg i dy deimladau di, rwy'n siwr. Roedd awyrgylch feirniadol yno hefyd – felly, heb sylweddoli hyn, rwy wedi bod yn ail-greu'r un awyrgylch, a dyma'r peth ola y byddwn am wneud, mewn gwirionedd. Rwy hyd yn oed wedi clywed fy hun yn dweud yr un pethau cas wrthyt ti ag oedd Mamgu yn ddweud [sic] wrthyf i, a heb fedru stopio fy hunan, a heb gael digon o nerth i dreio egluro wedyn – weithiau rwy'n meddwl bod rhyw ddiafol o'm mewn yn gwneud i mi ymddwyn fel hyn. Gwnaeth Mamgu i mi deimlo fy mod yn fethaint ar bob cyfrif – dim ond athrawes mewn ysgol. Dylwn wedi cael digon o gryfder i wneud beth oeddwn i am – trin llyfrau mewn rhyw ffordd. Mae braidd yn hwyr i sylweddoli nawr mai dysgu yw'r peth olaf y dylwn wneud, neu o leiaf, bod yn bennaeth adran a thrin pobl: rwy lawer hapusach ar hyn o bryd yn Rhydfelen am fy mod yn cael rhoi fy holl sylw ar beth rwy'n fwynhau [g]wneud sef paratoi llyfrau gosod i ddosbarthiadau 5 a 6, a pheidio poeni am y 'confrontations' *personnol. Ond wrth gwrs, yn nhermau gyrfa, rwy'n 'fethiant'.*

(I always had the feeling that it was only for my success in my work that I was respected – this is so similar to your feelings, I'm sure. There was a critical atmosphere there too – so, without realising it, I've been recreating the same atmosphere, and that's the last thing I would want to do, in truth. I've even heard myself saying the same nasty things to you as Mamgu said to me, without being able to stop myself, and without having enough strength to try to explain afterwards – sometimes I think that there's some devil inside me making me behave like this. Mamgu made me feel that I was a failure on all counts – only a schoolteacher. I should have had enough strength to do what I wanted to – dealing with books in some form. It's a bit late for me to realise now that teaching is the last thing I should do, or at least, being head of department and dealing with people: I'm much happier at the moment in Rhydfelen because I'm able to give my full attention to what I enjoy most, that is, preparing the set books for forms 5 and 6, and not worrying about personal 'confrontations'. But, of course, in career terms, I'm a 'failure'.)

Here the letter's sense of perspective starts to go askew. Surely being a schoolteacher is very far from being a failure, especially if you're the highly respected daughter of an equally well-thought-of headmaster?

Gan nad oeddwn wedi llwyddo i sefydlu perthynas dda gyda'm rhieni, roeddwn efallai wedi ceisio profi i'm hunan nad oeddwn yn fethiant llwyr drwy roi mwy mewn i'm plant fy hun nag oedd rhai pobl.

(Because I didn't succeed in establishing a good relationship with my parents I had perhaps tried to prove to myself that I wasn't a complete failure by putting more into my children than some people did.)

So we've suffered, not because you were cruel, but because you gave us more than other children had from their parents? Hm.

Roedd ein sefyllfa ni fel teulu yn unig hefyd – dim dadcu na mamgu na theulu agos i helpu a rhoi mwy o awyrgylch 'mynd a dod'. Dwy ddim wedi arfer cael pobl yn dod mewn a mas o'r tŷ, ac rwy'n ffeindio hyn yn anodd – rwy ofn nad wy'n gwybod sut i roi pryd o flaen ymwelwyr, sut i 'fihafio' – mae hwn yn chwerthinllyd i bobl eraill, rwy'n siwr; ond rwy ofn hefyd y byddant yn beirniadu'r anhrefn sydd yma – dwy jest yn methu copio a rhedeg ty'n 'deidi'. Rwy fel pe bawn yn gadael y glanhau i fod yn olaf a gwneud pethe eraill, a'r canlyniad yw nad yw'n cael ei wneud.

(Our situation as a family was lonely too – no grandfather or grandmother or close family to help and give more of an atmosphere of 'coming and going'. I'm not used to having people coming in and out of the house, and I find it hard – I'm afraid that I don't know how to put a meal in front of visitors, how to 'behave' – this is laughable to other people, I'm sure, but I'm also afraid that they'll judge the disorder here – I just can't cope with running a house 'tidily'. I seem to leave the cleaning till last and do other things, and the result is that it doesn't get done.)

Eryl knew very well how to be a good hostess – she was a fabulous cook. Her problem was that she worried about it too much to make it enjoyable for her.

Dyma fraslun i ti o rai o'r pethe rwy'n teimlo sy'n gyfrifol am y sefyllfa bresennol, i ryw raddau. Mae'n biti mewn ffordd hefyd dy fod di'n gwneud Saesneg gan bod cymaint o ddiddordeb gen i yn y pwnc – pe baet ti'n gwneud 'Computer Studies' *byddwn i ddim yn gwybod beth sy'n mynd ymlaen ac felly'n poeni llai!*

(This is an outline of some of the things that I feel are responsible for the present situation, to some extent.

It's a pity in a way as well that you're doing English because I have so much interest in the subject – if you were doing 'Computer Studies' I wouldn't know what was going on and therefore worry less!)

So, Eryl was mean because she was concerned.

Gobeithio na fyddi di'n grac am hyn, ond ffonion ni Dr McKendrick ddoe – roeddem bron drysu ddim yn gwybod beth i wneud – dim 'checkio' arnat ti oedd bwriad hyn, ond jest i ddatgan ein pryder a gofyn a oedd unrhywbeth y dylem wneud. Buom ddim ond yn siarad rhyw 5 munud ac mi roedd hi yn siarad yn uchel iawn amdanat ti fel person a dweud dy fod yn berson arbennig iawn. Roedd hi'n meddwl dy fod wedi gwneud y penderfyniad iawn i gario mlaen – byddai'n fwy anodd ail-gydio mewn pethau wedyn, a bod gyda pobl flwyddyn ar dy ôl di. Cyn hynny roeddwn ni'n teimlo efallai bod gwendid corfforol ddim wedi bod yn help, a byddai'n well i di gryfhau'n iawn cyn mynd nol i'r frwydr. Ond wedyn, byddai'n ddiflas i ti adre a phawb arall bant.

*Y peth i'w wneud i'w [sic] gwneud y gorau gallu di, a bod yn esmwyth dy feddwl na fyddwn ots gennym ni beth fydd dy ganlyniadau *cyhyd a dy fod di yn <u>teimlo'n</u> iawn unwaith eto – dyna'r peth pwysig.*

**Os wyt am fframio hwn a'i gadw'n barchus, mi arwydda i fe, gyda Dad yn dyst!*

Pan fyddi di'n dod adre, mi wna i fy ngore –

(I hope you're not cross about this, but we phoned Dr McKendrick [my moral tutor] yesterday – we nearly flummoxed about what to do – our intention wasn't to 'check' on you but just to declare our concern and ask if there was anything we should do. We only spoke for about 5 minutes and she was very sensible. She talked very highly about you as a person and said that you're a very special person; also that your work is very good. She thought that you had made the right decision to carry on – it would be harder to take hold of things after, and to be with people the year after you. Before that I felt that perhaps physical weakness [from the glandular fever] hadn't been a help, and that it would be better for you to get strong properly before returning to the fray. But then, it would be miserable for you at home with everybody else away.

The thing to do is to do your best, and to be easy in your mind that we won't mind what your results are, *as long as you <u>feel</u> better once again – that's the important thing.

* If you want to frame this and keep it respectable, I'll sign it, with Dad as a witness!

When you come home, I'll do my best –)

The letter then continues with the truism that we hurt those we love the most and that the menopause hasn't helped the situation. My student self is highly reassured by this letter but, reading it now, I can't help noticing that Eryl doesn't even mention her hostility to R or acknowledge his strong support of me through this time. Yet again, he's being excluded, even though he's central to my life.

—An apology here somewhere wouldn't have gone amiss.

Just how much difference my pleas for better treatment have made is shown by a note Gwilym slips in with Eryl's letter which bodes ill for future tolerance. Some friendly girls from my year have invited me to share a college house with them the following academic year. My parents aren't keen and will not trust me that this is a good proposal:

Ŷnglyn a'r syniad o rannu tŷ – gobeithio nad oes brys a chawn amser i drafod hyn, oherwydd mae yna snags efallai nad wyt yn rhagweld.

> (About the idea of sharing a house – I hope that there's no rush and that we have time to discuss this, because there are snags that perhaps you don't foresee.)

I've been driven to the end of my tether, stated the case for my freedom and still they think they know better. I take up the offer of a place in the shared house on Girton Corner for the following year and it gives me my happiest time in Cambridge. As it is, I decide that I'm not well enough to continue with my studies and 'degrade', in order to recover at home.

When I return to Cardiff, the only thing that has changed at home is that I've won the right to smoke in my bedroom. R is still not welcome. One day, he rings and Eryl puts the phone down on him, without telling me he's called. Friends tell me of an artist looking for a lodger in town, so I rent a room and move out, which causes a terrible scene. They tell me that I'm showing them up, that it's a waste of money, so I get a job and do it anyway.

Having returned to my studies, two years later, I graduate with a double first, apply for and am awarded a Harkness Fellowship to study in America. On graduation day, I have more cause than many to celebrate, given how much I've survived. My parents and sister attend. After I've received my degree in the Senate House, I want to wait outside to see my friends emerge in their turn and rejoice with them. A sullen Eryl throws a tantrum and insists that we go back to college for lunch. It's my day, not hers but she ruins the occasion and my father lets her do it.

Shortly afterwards, I leave for the States to become a poet again or, perhaps, for the first time.

Chapter 8
REMISSIONS

I never lived with my parents again. In the years to come, there was no magical transformation into a harmonious family. I survived, but discovered that you never fully recover.

After leaving college, I spend three years in America, trying everything that comes my way. New York is full of people who don't like their families and who, therefore, construct an alternative kin structure. Most importantly to me, I start writing for the first time without interference. I begin by writing in Welsh and translating poems, which doesn't give me the range of expression that I want. I'm not performing for school competitions any more but meeting and being taught by world-class poets, for whom poetry matters before nearly everything. The contrast between their work and mine is mortifying but their company deeply encouraging. I don't yet have the words or technique to produce decent work, but I learn how writers live.

After a PEN reading one night by an Eastern European poet, I find myself in a cellar bar with him. We drink ourselves sober and stay up all night. I tell him that I'm not going to a seminar (full of famous people) the following day as I have to work on a poem. Fixing bright eyes on me, he says, 'You're perfect!'

It takes a long time for poems of any value to come, but he didn't mean that: his comment was about a fundamental orientation towards art. I don't see him again for decades until we were both taking part in a festival. By then, I've published widely in Welsh and also in English. We become firm friends.

Living in New York is lonely and I have very little money. Gwilym offers to send a cheque; I thank him but refuse. He reflects that it's a good thing to know how to live on no money. I phone home another time on my birthday, desperate for some comfort. I must have said something Eryl didn't like. She hangs up on me. The sound of the dial tone was a blow to the side of my head. In contrast, a friend of mine recently told me that, when her children call her, she never brings the conversation to a close, but lets them decide when they've finished talking with her. Such kindness makes me want to cry with longing.

I eventually return to the UK to do a doctorate on literary forgeries. Having been pushed into so many false positions of my own, I'm interested in what drives writers to embrace bold strategies of concealment and invention. At last, my poems start appearing in magazines and I'm invited to give readings. I graduate and return to Cardiff to work as a researcher for a television company.

Over the years, I'd struggled with my mental health and become addicted to alcohol, which deepens my depression and loneliness to previously inconceivable levels. Eventually, suffering from the shakes and unable to think of anything other than how to find the next bottle, I become desperate enough to ask for help and sober up. Around the same time, I meet Leighton. It's an unconventional relationship, with an age gap of twenty-four years between us. We don't share political or religious views but we trust each other implicitly. Being together makes us happier than either of us has ever been. He's ferociously intelligent and possesses a dog's intuitive instinct about people. He's a plain speaker, like my old friend, Mwnci. I have the great good fortune to be married to a person who puts my welfare ahead of his own, as I put his ahead of mine.

As ever, Eryl is hostile. She's heard me talking about a new friend, Leighton, who'd been in the Merchant Navy. Even though I'm thirty years old, she intrudes: she hopes I haven't, surely I haven't been so foolish as to get *involved*? She then insinuates he's been a sailor, I don't know where he's been, he might give me the clap.

'Too late!' I inform her.

It has been thirty years since Leighton had left the sea.

Her attitude is no better when I invite my parents to meet Leighton. Superficially, the encounter seems to be going well but, while I'm out refilling the teapot, Eryl turns to Leighton and says that she's appalled that her daughter has ended up with someone 'like him'. He doesn't rise to the bait or tell me this for decades.

Far from improving, over the years, Eryl's hostility towards me became more overt. I was an adult now, and had a choice whether or not to put up with it. Leighton and I had been living together for a year when we decided to get married. Eryl refused to come to our wedding. Gwilym brought the news and wept with helplessness at our kitchen table for failing, as ever, to persuade her to be reasonable. I'd have thought more of him if he'd left her to her own devices and refused to engage with such theatrics. Of course, she changed her mind at the eleventh hour and started adding guests to the list. Just when I thought nothing Eryl did could surprise me any more, I asked her if I could sleep in my parents' house on the night before the wedding and she said no. I told a friend about it.

'It's an animal thing', he explained, 'she's a bitch running a rival off her patch.'

Eryl did come to the wedding, dressed in black and thoroughly enjoyed the day, swanning around as if she'd organised the whole thing. When we went to Goa for our honeymoon, Eryl demanded the key to our house. I refused. On our return, she didn't speak to us for three weeks. Who in their right mind gives an abusive mother the key to their first real home and permission to trespass there too? Not me. I was so used to being sent to Coventry that it didn't bother me at all. In fact, it was a relief.

After a few years, Gwilym began to visit me and Leighton regularly on a Saturday morning, which gave me great pleasure. In a moment of folly, I mentioned this to Eryl and the visits promptly stopped.

So, why did I carry on having contact with my parents? One benefit of having been a nightshade daughter is that it's forced me think very hard about imagination and desire. I'm a writer who doesn't trust the imagination because the gaslit brain, primed to believe other people's fantasies, can easily become a hall of mirrors. I knew that my desire for good parents dovetailed with the fiction that I was a bad daughter who needed to be corrected or blocked out. My ability to judge right and wrong – in myself and in others – has been irreparably damaged by the abusive parts of my upbringing. Despite therapy, spiritual disciplines and being a fully grown adult with experience in the world, my default setting is to feel that I'm wrong and other people – including those who wish me harm (especially them!) – are right and that I should, therefore, do what they want.

The big difference between this voluntary contact and my childhood was that I could walk out at any time. I was in charge of my own self-esteem and no longer hostage to Eryl's moods. Now it was a fight between equals. Leighton, with great wisdom, let me conduct my own battles with Eryl, thus keeping our marriage out of that dynamic which had destroyed so much in the earlier part of my life. Eryl was, with good reason, afraid of him and never pushed her luck. In fact, he could twist her round his little finger with his charm and forthrightness. She had finally met her match. During the last few weeks of her life, when I had to be away to work, Leighton would call and deliver home-cooked meals to Eryl. He knew exactly what she could enjoy and she told him, one day, with humour, that he was 'nearly wonderful'. And yet, he recalls, when Marian phoned to say that she was coming over, Eryl dismissed him, saying he had to go. He got the message that Marian was preferred loud and clear.

In the end, keeping in touch with my parents and looking after them until their deaths wasn't generosity in me, but a matter of survival. Knowing that I'd behaved as well as I possibly could and had no reason to reproach myself as a daughter was the best way to be free from the ongoing psychic damage their oppression had inflicted on me. I was playing the long game. Being kind was my revenge.

In short, Eryl continued to be Eryl, which I still found outrageous. Over the years, I visited Megan and Bill at Hafod y Coed many times and Megan and I became very close. Before marrying Leighton, I took him there on approval. Megan and I both liked and loved each other. For me, she was proof that coming from a miserable childhood didn't mean I was doomed to stay in it as an adult. Megan and Bill visited Wales a couple of times in the later years of their lives. They always stayed with me. Megan declared:

'I get on better with you than I do with my own sister!'

Eryl wouldn't even have them round to her house for a cup of tea. She was, I believe, ashamed of the house which was gloomy, run down. Once time, when she'd been in hospital, Leighton and I cleaned, to cheer her up when she came home. She was mortified and angry with us.

On Megan's last visit to Wales, I invited Eryl and Gwilym round to see them at my house. I put an arm round the sisters, like a bridge for an awkward photo, but there was no reconciliation between them.

L to R: Megan, Gwyneth, Eryl

When Megan died, I was bereft. Eryl sent not one word of condolence to her nephews. She was, at least, consistent in her hatred and no hypocrite. My cousins gave me the gold-nugget earrings that Bill had given my aunt. They are a touchstone.

I came to appreciate Eryl's bluntness because, bruising though it could be, it meant that I always knew where I stood with her. I remember two instances of Eryl softening towards me. The first happened when I was at work and Leighton at home. We'd now been married for some years. Eryl knocked the door, as she was out walking her dog. Leighton invited her in, but she refused.

'I just came to say that I've never seen my daughter so happy.'

Then she left. She knew, of course, that Leighton would relay the message to me.

Eryl lived in her own house right until the last two weeks of her life. I called to bring food and check on her one day, only to find that she'd had an accident with her bowels. I cleaned her and sorted her out, trying to disperse her shame ('It's only poo, you've dealt with plenty of mine') but this was a deep humiliation for her. A few days later, she told Leighton – not me – that I'd been very good. It would have killed her to tell me to my face. I didn't need her second-hand approval by then, it had come decades too late.

—She pushed her self-hatred on to you.
—That's a bitter inheritance.
—If you accept it.

Was I a bad daughter to her? I don't think so. I did everything that I could to please her, except when that risked destroying myself. I would not see her suffer wrong or discomfort if I could prevent it. As for this book, I'm sure that Eryl would say that it would kill her – if she weren't already dead. I'm not proud that I had to write it, nor pleased by what I've understood as a result of finishing it. However, this sustained act of attention, over years, in all kinds of emotional states, good years, bad years, business and ill health, is the best kind of love I can offer Eryl: the drive to understand and be truthful. I'm aware that I'm the sardonic child who looks with a questioning eye. If I'm hard now it's because I couldn't be when I was growing up. If I'm soft now, it's because I understand and pity my mother still. I chose to stay part of this family anyway, which is its own description of love, though I might not call it that.

I've heard of a stage of enlightenment in which the Zen student feels as though there's a red-hot iron ball and it's stuck in her throat. She can neither digest it nor cough it up. The impediment gives the postulant no rest nor peace of mind. Nothing will wear her obsession away. Writing this story, I've felt like a python that's swallowed a goat and, its jaw dislocated, is extended way beyond its normal shape, intent on nothing but the process of digestion.

Writing this has been brutally hard work, and where has it got me? All I have is the glimmer of a shape resulting from a long act of looking but that is not nothing. There's no triumph over adversity in this story. I've fought against this inheritance tooth and nail but it still makes me ill. Dwelling on my Nightshade inheritance is unbearable but, in finishing this book, I lose Nightshade Eryl for ever. Now I'm stuck between a double grief – for what was and what wasn't – and an even stronger drive to be free. I feel no confessional catharsis, no triumphalism at having survived.

People talk today as if writing creatively were an entirely benign activity. I know in my bones – having had Eryl's interference poison my poetry for me at source – that there are dark, uninnocent aspects to the process. Welsh myth gives an account of how poison and poetic talent are related.

The last project I worked on before becoming crippled by migraine a few years ago was a translation, with Rowan Williams, of *The Book of Taliesin*. For medieval poets, Taliesin (who was historical), became a mythical figure, about whom an origin story for poetry was invented. Here are the bare bones of the tale. Ceridwen is the mother of a very ugly son, Morfran Afagddu ('pitch-black sea-raven'). To make up for this, the enchantress brews a broth that, when drunk, will make him a poet. She employs a servant, Gwion

Bach ('Little Gwion'), to tend to the fire under the cauldron. By accident, a drop of the scalding potion falls on his hand, which he brings to his mouth, thus receiving the talent that's intended for Ceridwen's son. The witch is furious and hunts him down in an elaborate shape-shifting contest. Gwion turns himself into a hare but she pursues him as a greyhound, he becomes a fish and she an otter, he transforms into a bird and she into a hawk. The chase ends when Gwion, in the form of a grain of wheat, is swallowed by Ceridwen in the form of a hen. She subsequently gives birth to him and abandons the child to the river and, eventually, the sea in a leather bag which is a second womb.

I'm Gwion who, by accident, gets in the way. For me, the key to the myth is that Gwion's name may mean 'a little prototypic poison'. The servant boy – destined to become a great poet – is, at the beginning, the troublesome being who comes between an enchantress and her will to act on the world by magic. In the end, he can't not be caught by Ceridwen's superior powers. He's digested but, most importantly, he survives to live his own life as the poet Taliesin. The renaming shows how radically the pursuit has changed him – for the better – and how inventive he had to be to avoid being obliterated. This catches the only advantage, perhaps, of being hunted so hard: it trains you to be nimble and, hopefully, more alert than your pursuer.

In a letter written to John Aubrey in 1694, the Welsh metaphysical poet Henry Vaughan recounts a local story of a shepherd who falls asleep and has a dream in which he sees 'a beautifull young man with a garland of green leafs vpon his head, & an hawk vpon his fist'. The god eventually:

> lett the hawk fly att him, w^ch^ (he dreamt) gott into his mouth & inward parts, & suddenly awaked in a great fear & consternation: butt possessed with such a vein, or gift of poetrie, that he left the sheep & went about the Countrey, making Songs vpon all occasions, and came to be the most famous Bard in all the Countrey in his time.

This muse is a hunter, as is mine. Unleashed, it comes back with its talons bloody but bearing food. Being hunted makes you nimble and I've discovered that I have a survival instinct so strong that I've escaped the worst not once but many times. My parents wanted me to stay in thrall to them, which completely backfired. Fighting them has made me fearless. Having been forced to bow down once, I won't yield to anyone if I don't think it's right. I've been inoculated by this formative experience against some other hostile organisms. This isn't to my parents' credit but down to my own reaction to them. I can't bear emotion manufactured in the interests of one party alone. I will not say things to please another person unless I believe them to be true. I'm determined to stick with what only I can know about my life, no matter how much others try to shout me out of it, otherwise, I'm lost. These are not inconsiderable tools in a world where the performance of fantasy is often given precedence before honesty with self and others.

This is my achievement, not my parents': I'm unbiddable and am going to be a formidable old woman.

In psychology and self-help circles, everyone's very keen for you to forgive but I don't see why. Simone Weil was right when she said that forgiveness can only be attempted when the full extent of an offence is known. Before writing this book, I hadn't allowed myself to calculate this price to me. What my parents did to me was worse than I'd allowed myself to remember. Now that I've looked in such detail at my life with Eryl and Gwilym, I de-forgive them. You can't forgive people who think they've done nothing wrong. Eryl never asked for forgiveness, and I never gave it, so I can't hope for William Blake's vision of forgiveness, jotted down in his notebook: 'Throughout all Eternity / I forgive you you forgive me'.

In her novel, *Lolly Willowes*, Sylvia Townsend Warner's heroine of the same name is, like me, slow to rebellion but then single-minded. She moves away from a tyrannical family to live an independent life in a pagan village. She doesn't make her peace with her tormentors but offers a broader understanding:

> There was no question of forgiving them. She had not, in any case, a forgiving nature; and the injury they had done her was not done by them. If she were to start forgiving she must needs forgive Society, the Law, the Church, the History of Europe, the Old Testament, great-great-aunt Salome and her prayer-book, the Bank of England, Prostitution, the Architect of Apsley Terrace, and half a dozen other useful props of civilisation. All she could do was to go on forgetting them. But now she was able to forget them without flouting them by her forgetfulness.

I wish that I could make Eryl and Gwilym simply people of their historical period but that won't wash. There were some parents who were much worse than them but many of the same background who bestowed on their children that sense of being loved that grants a lifetime's confidence and emotional security.

In the end, I'm not my mother's judge but part of my parents' stories, as they are of mine. I hope that this account is less of a condemnation than a holding to account. But a blanket exoneration is not compatible with my own self-respect. Eryl's had enough of my time. It's time to 'forget without flouting' and move on, with Lolly Willowes, into the pagan woods.

Eryl looked after Gwilym right up the end of his life and when he was admitted to the hospice, in 2013, she was exhausted. As he was lying comatose but still able to hear us, Eryl began to discuss organising the funeral. I briskly changed the subject. There's a difference between being unsentimental and being entirely without tact at a life-turning moment. My sister and I left Eryl and Gwilym alone to say goodbye and then we took her home. That was the last she saw of him. My sister and I waited the long week with Gwilym until he died.

—I don't think their marriage was happy, do you Gwyneth?

I once told Eryl that she was lucky Dad hadn't left her. I still think that she might have been better off with a different husband. After Gwilym had died, and Eryl was living alone, more than half blind, in a big house, I asked her if she was lonely. She said that she wasn't but mentioned that she wished that Gwilym had hugged her more. As I left, that evening, I gave her a hug and did so every time I visited from then on. This embrace surprised us both. I was the giant now, Mam had shrunk with age. Why was I comforting a woman who'd caused me such grief and had shown no remorse about doing so?

I hugged her for the delightful letters that she sent me daily when, aged ten, I was homesick at youth camp in Llangrannog. I hugged her for the time that I was late for school and she plonked me on the luggage rack of her Raleigh bike and pedalled like hell for the bus stop. I hugged her for trying and failing to comb out the cobbles in my long curly hair, as I'm trying to disentangle the ways that we're knotted together now. I hugged her for sending me money so that I could buy freesias while I was sitting my finals at Cambridge. This late decision to embrace was like gathering a bouquet of nettles to myself. If you hold them closely and firmly enough, they say they don't hurt. Each time I hugged her the currents between us changed direction. Eryl patted my back, as if winding a baby, or consoling a child that I had been.

So the consoler becomes the consoled in this unexpected slow-dance with my nightshade mother.

Towards the end of Eryl's life, when my sister and I were struggling to care for her at home and were exhausted, Eryl kept on refusing to have carers come to help her. She was polite to them but would not even let them make her a cup of tea. One evening, I was so frustrated that I withheld my *cwtsh*, just that once. But I regret that now, I should have cuddled her anyway.

To my mind, there's no difference at all between a religious practice and practising an art. The aim of both is to transform the self into – what? I can't know, but I listen to the tiny daily promptings that replaces a phrase with one that's more fitting. There's no grand revelation, just a drip-feed of suggestions, adjustments. It's a stripping of the pleasing lie for the less fallacious, the statement whose sense and aptness will hold. The shorthand for this is beauty. It's modest, remorseless and, like the excavation of reality, it's a life-and-death matter.

In *The Go-Between*, L. P. Hartley describes the deadly nightshade growing in a glasshouse, the mother plant that has poisoned young Leo's imagination, as uncanny in its relation to time:

> This plant seemed to be up to something, to be carrying on a questionable traffic with itself. There was no harmony, no proportion in its parts. It exhibited all the stages of its development at once. It was young, middle-aged, and old at the same time … It invited and yet repelled inspection, as if it was harbouring some shady secret which it yet wanted to know. Outside the shed, twilight was darkening the air, but inside it was already night, night which the plant had gathered to itself.

Later, Leo notes that 'In some way it wanted me, I felt, just as I wanted it; and the fancy took me that it wanted me as an ingredient, and would have me'.

In her attempt to make me palatable to herself, my nightshade mother nearly destroyed me, a process which my father allowed to happen not once, but many times. This was deeply wounding.

As for the house, will Leighton and I decide to stay? He wants to, I don't. For me, it's far from being ideal but I'm no longer living in my mother's house. She's living in mine. She visits, but she's not invited to stay. Far more important is that Leighton and I have made a home in which young Gwyneth would be happy to dwell. I leave her to her own devices. And Mwnci sits on my desk. His face, made of velvet, is rather worn, but we smile at each other and know what we know. He averts his gaze but he has my ear. I consult him often.

Serious ill health brings back the traumas of the past, as if they'd just happened. Totally unexpectedly, the crippling migraines have receded, making enjoying daily life, rather than enduring it, possible again. This is due to new medications on the market combined with a strict no carb, no sugar diet and, crucially, the support of other migraine sufferers. Facing the full brunt of the past has certainly lightened the burden. Somatic therapy has enabled me to use my imagination to find safe places in my body, to which I can retreat when the past decides to attack again. I had not dared hope for this new freedom from pain and despair. From now on, I'll concentrate on removing that helmet of migraine and emotional pain. I'll take off my thinking head and, instead, forget who I was and concentrate on what I am now.

Chronic illness has changed my ambitions. They're both larger and smaller. Still convalescent, I'd like to get physically fit again. I want to plant some Black-Eyed Susan (Rudbeckia), so that its yellow-irised eyes can cheer these last days of autumn.

I've found a member of the nightshade family with which I can do business. On my walks, I've been noticing a humble plant that grows on a certain bend in the path. I'd took it to be ground elder but found that it's called enchanter's-nightshade. I look at the flower under a magnifying glass and recoil in surprise. The flowers are pink and look like heart-shaped butterflies pinned to the stems. Richard Mabey describes the plant well:

> From a distance it is drab, stark, small-flowered, and haunts what Gerard described as 'obscure and darke places' – damp woods, hedge-banks, heavy soil in garden corners and the foot of old walls.

This flower's a wolf in sheep's clothing. It's not part of the nightshade family at all, but, as Mabey summarises, a 'modest member of the willowherbs'. A sixteenth-century Flemish botanist misidentified it and then Parisian botanists fantasised that this was the plant that the witch Circe in *The Odyssey* used to turn Odysseus's crew into animals, giving it the Latin name *Circaea lutetiana* (meaning the Parisian Circe). In Welsh, the plant's called simply 'Llysiau'r Swynwr' (the 'Enchanter's Plant').

It's a false enchanter. Its lack of showiness, its insistence on putting out humble flowers – not at all how flamboyant nightshade blossoms should be – gives it the virtue and power of humility.

Like the deadly nightshade, this plant too was absent from my childhood herbarium. I'll add it to my repertoire now and note that, according to the Woodland Trust, it can be used to treat wounds and as a flavouring in Austrian tea and, most endearing of all, that in Scotland it's an aphrodisiac. From now on, it's my favourite nightshade.

Nightshade isn't a climbing plant, nor does it entangle other vegetation, though it may tower over it. A healthy family dynamic is all about connection, but one which permits all its members enough freedom to be autonomous through choice. The aim isn't separation but free will, within the bounds of duty and love. That's not what I experienced, but suffocation. I could give bitterness for bitterness, or I can oppose with as much love as I can muster, which I did from the start. In the end, it comes down to temperament.

Behind me I see a chimera plant, a hybrid of nightshade mother and daughter. Its branches reach across years into many versions of Eryl and myself at different ages. There I am, dripping with glass-covered milk in a porch, crying with rage in my bedroom, hearing the imagined burglars breaking into my room, thinking of killing myself. Here's Mwnci laughing with me in the shade and, his counterpart, Leighton, shaking the plant so that the poison berries rain down, untasted. And here am I, too, reaching out to those younger Gwyneths and pulling them out from the shouting, and the rage. Where will we go together now? When this memoir releases me, who will I be? I have no idea.

Now that is exciting.

ACKNOWLEDGEMENTS

This book has been a lifetime in the making.

I'll start with the most important debt first. Not only has my husband Leighton seen me suffer over the years, he's paid a price for that pain but been utterly steadfast on my side. He's also encouraged me tirelessly throughout the writing of *Nightshade Mother* and, most importantly, always told me the truth especially when I didn't want to hear it.

My sister Marian's experience of my parents was different from mine. I've talked about her as little as possible not because she wasn't and isn't important to me but in order to protect her privacy. Despite hating the fact that I'm publishing this book, she's read it, has shared her comments honestly. We will never agree about our parents but have decided to continue being sisters and for that generosity I'm grateful.

James MacDonald Lockhart, my agent, was, after Leighton, the first reader of *Nightshade Mother* and his 'getting it' and his calm support and hard work throughout made the trauma of revisiting these experiences much easier.

Due to my childhood experiences, I trust very few people with sight of my writing, but I'm lucky in having been able to show the first draft to some excellent readers. M. Wynn Thomas grasped it immediately, when I was in great doubt, and his comments gave me courage to persist. Juliet Grayson was also an early and essential reader; those who know her work will understand how her friendship made survival possible for me when I was extremely hard-pushed.

I'm proud to enjoy the friendship of an array of formidable intellectual women, who all took time and trouble to comment extensively on the draft and to save me from myself multiple times. I'm a better person and writer for knowing Isobel Armstrong, Susan Stewart, and Laurie Patten. alice hiller helped at a crucial moment and is uniquely placed to understand a book like this. Alice Entwistle, Rhianwen Daniel and Sioned Puw Rowlands were also early readers and I thank them for their forbearance in letting me inflict it on them. Clare Shaw's understanding carried me through a tough time.

I'm also grateful to Megan Hayes, my mother's cousin, for reading what must have been difficult material. My cousin Joe Tanner also checked the American section and corrected information about his parents, Megan and Bill Tanner.

I prepared to write this book through a period of serious illness and am deeply grateful to the Royal Literary Fund for emergency financial support. I also owe a great debt to the Society of Authors both for grants from its Contingency Fund and also an Authors' Foundation Arthur Welton Award, which allowed me to complete the writing.

Finally, I'd like to thank all at Calon for their care and sensitivity while preparing *Nightshade Mother* for publication; they have eased the path of an unusually difficult book for me. I'm grateful to all those listed below for their commitment, enthusiasm and creative flair:

Editorial: Amy Feldman, Abbie Headon, Caleb Woodbridge, Elin Nesta Lewis, Paula Clarke-Bain and Caroline Goldsmith
Cover design: Jason Anscomb
Text design: Agnes Graves
Production: Steven Goundrey and Adam Burns
Press and Publicity: Georgia Winstone, Elin Williams, Maria Vassilopoulos and Ruth Killick

I'm greatly in your debt.

REFERENCES

Epigraphs

Nicholas Culpeper, *Culpeper's Complete Herbal* (London, 1816), p. 252.

Emily Dickinson, *The Poems of Emily Dickinson: Reading Edition*, ed. R.W Franklin, (Cambridge, Mass.: Belknap, 1999), p. 377.

Prelude: The 'Powers of Love Reversed'

John Cheever, 'Goodbye, My Brother', *Collected Stories* (London, 1990), p. 33.

Edward St Aubyn, *At Last* (London: Picador, 2012), p. 166.

Charles Dickens, *The Old Curiosity Shop* (London, 1867), p. 330.

William Faulkner, *Absalom, Absalom!* (Harmondsworth: Penguin Books, 1980), p. 113.

Georges Simenon, *Letter to my Mother*, trans. Ralph Manheim (London: Penguin Classics, 2018), p. 17.

TOXINS

Shakespeare, *Cymbeline*, Act I, Sc. VI, ll. 10–16.

Chapter 1: Invalid

Gwyneth Lewis, '"My father was distant …"', *Chaotic Angels* (Tarset: Bloodaxe Books, 2005), p. 152.

Gwyneth Lewis, 'Yr Etifedd', *Tair Mewn Un: Cerddi Detholedig* ('Three in One: Selected Poems') (Swansea: Barddas, 2005), p. 83, translated by the author.

Chapter 2: Mistaken Identities

Genesis 27:27

Simone Weil, *Gravity and Grace*, trans. Gustave Thibon (London: Routledge and Kegan Paul, 1963), p. 117.

Gwyneth Lewis, 'Llyfr Geirfa fy Nhad', *Treiglo* ('Mutating') (Swansea: Barddas, 2017), p. 63.

Chapter 3: Damnation

Rhodd Mam, (Caernarfon: Llyfrfa'r Methodistiaid Calfinaidd, 1860), pp. 24–5.

Michel Serres, *The Parasite* (Baltimore: Johns Hopkins University Press, 1982), p. 231.

Benjamin Spock, *Dr Benjamin Spock's Baby and Child Care* (London: New English Library, 1975), p. 235.

Chapter 4: Witnesses

Gwyneth Lewis, *Sunbathing in the Rain: A Cheerful Book about Depression* (London: Fourth Estate, 2006), pp. 33–5.

Chapter 5: Top

L. P. Hartley, *The Go-Between* (London: Macmillan Collector's Library, 2017), pp. 51–2.

ANTIDOTES

Shakespeare, *Cymbeline*, Act I, Sc. VI, ll. 33–6, 42–4.

Chapter 6: Two Kinds of Elsewhere

The Etymologies of Isidore of Seville, trans. Stephen A. Barney et al. (Cambridge: Cambridge University Press, 2014), p. 114.

Chapter 7: Crisis

Gwyneth Lewis, *Sunbathing in the Rain: A Cheerful Book about Depression* (London: Fourth Estate, 2006), p. 45.

Chapter 8: Remissions

Henry Vaughan, *The Works of Henry Vaughan*, vol. II, ed. Donald R. Dickson, Alan Rudrum and Robert Wilcher (Oxford: Oxford University Press, 2018), p. 811.

Sylvia Townsend Warner, *Lolly Willowes* (London: Penguin Books, 2020), p. 98.

L. P. Hartley, *The Go-Between* (London: Macmillan Collector's Library, 2017), pp. 239–40, 299.

Richard Mabey, *Flora Britannica* (London: Chatto & Windus, 1998), p. 238.

The author wishes to thank Cyhoeddiadau Barddas for kind permission to reproduce 'Yr Etifedd' from *Tair Mewn Un* (2005) and 'Llyfr Geirfa fy Nhad' from *Treiglo* (2017), and Bloodaxe Books for kind permission to reproduce '"My father was distant ..."' from *Chaotic Angels* (2005).